KINANGIOLOGY

Co-working With the Angels to Heal Emotions

First published by O Books, 2009

O Books is an imprint of John Hunt Publishing Ltd., The Bothy, Deershot Lodge, Park Lane, Ropley,
Hants, SO24 0BE, UK
office1@o-books.net
www.o-books.net

Distribution in:	South Africa
	Alternative Books
UK and Europe	altbook@peterhyde.co.za
Orca Book Services	Tel: 021 555 4027 Fax: 021 447 1430
orders@orcabookservices.co.uk	
Tel: 01202 665432 Fax: 01202 666219	Text copyright Sue Vaughan 2009
Int. code (44)	
	Design: Stuart Davies
USA and Canada	Illustrations: Sue Vaughan
NBN	
custserv@nbnbooks.com	ISBN: 978 1 84694 186 3
Tel: 1 800 462 6420 Fax: 1 800 338 4550	

Australia and New Zealand
Brumby Books
sales@brumbybooks.com.au
Tel: 61 3 9761 5535 Fax: 61 3 9761 7095

Far East (offices in Singapore, Thailand,
Hong Kong, Taiwan)
Pansing Distribution Pte Ltd
kemal@pansing.com
Tel: 65 6319 9939 Fax: 65 6462 5761

A CIP catalogue record for this book is available
from the British Library.

Printed by Chris Fowler International
www.chrisfowler.com

O Books operates a distinctive and ethical publishing philosophy in
all areas of its business, from its global network of authors to
production and worldwide distribution.

This book is produced on FSC certified stock, within ISO14001
standards. The printer plants sufficient trees each year through
the Woodland Trust to absorb the level of emitted carbon in
its production.

KINANGIOLOGY

Co-working With the Angels to Heal Emotions

Sue Vaughan

BOOKS

Winchester, UK
Washington, USA

CONTENTS

Dedicated to
Aurora

ACKNOWLEDGEMENTS

I would like to acknowledge Dawn Brumham. Without her help and encouragement, this book may never have progressed from a course manual into a book. Thank you Martyn, as always, for your love, support and patience. For all those clients and students who asked "Is there a book about this stuff?" Thank you because finally here it is. Thanks also to all my unseen helpers, as always, my recognition and gratitude for your inspiration, love and blessings.

PREFACE

Kinangiology (KA) combines the practice of kinesiology (muscle testing) to communicate and co-work with the angels to clear emotional blocks, program positive affirmations and eliminate phobias. The purpose of this book is to give you a powerful toolbox of useful techniques you can make use of to help yourself and others to make decisions, clear the clutter that may be blocking progress towards living a more rewarding life and discover the joy of co-working with the angels.

KA can be used by literally anyone and anywhere whether you are at home amongst friends and family or in a more formal environment such as a traditional surgery or clinic. There are hundreds of different types of kinesiology: Applied Kinesiology, Clinical Kinesiology, Health Kinesiology, Touch for Health and so on. KA would blend seamlessly with each one. KA has also proved to blend excellently with other disciplines such as Hypnosis, Neuro Linguistic Programming (NLP), Clinical Nutrition, Osteopathy and Physiotherapy.

However, I have also noticed over the years that quite a large percentage of people attending KA workshops are people simply wanting to learn the KA system of techniques and approaches in order that they can replicate the benefits with their family and friends away from the workshop.

Whether you choose to dip in and out of this book, read it out of curiosity (you'll find the case histories fascinating), use it on a regular basis as a manual of techniques or pick and program one of the positive affirmations for the day, that is up to you. You may be one of those people that will read straight through the book and then go through it again to work through the techniques or you may do it as you go. Which ever way you choose to use this book, it is laid out so that it will be easy for you to access whether you are completely new to these ideas or already somewhat

1

familiar with them.

In Part I, I have given some information about the angels and my personal experience of my connection with them. You will also find meditations and ideas you can use to connect with them yourself. Part II gives you all the basics to getting started with KA; muscle testing, silent questioning, how to invite the angels to co-work with you and how to check they are all there.

Part III contains instructions on how to do the actual techniques of KA starting with a chapter on what it is and how it developed. I have given a case history for each of the techniques to illustrate them in action. You can see from the contents list which technique will be described. For example, Chapter 12: Programming Affirmations will show you how to choose and program positive affirmations. Chapter 14, Phobia Clearing Technique, will obviously be devoted to phobias. Chapter 15: The Emotional Clearing Technique, will explain how to find out where there are emotional blocks lodged in the body, what the emotion is, who/what caused it and how to clear them. Muscle testing can be used on your pets, children and those people not strong enough to test directly on them by using someone else as a surrogate so there is some tips on this as well as dowsing in Part III.

There are more case histories in the Appendixes *and*, of course, all the names have been changed to preserve anonymity. There is also, for those of a scientific nature, an explanation of the mind/body/spirit connection; the limbic system, Psychoneuroimmunology (PNI) which is a study of how the body's immune system is affected by emotions and an A-Z of how emotions can affect different parts of the body. I have also added an explanation of allergy testing and correction.

As KA uses muscle testing, you will need someone to practise on. Family and friends will be the usual "victims". Many of the people that attend KA workshops team up in pairs or small groups to practise the techniques. One of my students who has become a close friend lives nearby and she and I swap KA sessions on a regular basis. You may want to find a friend with whom you can work through the meditations and techniques so that you may practise together. It will be a wonderful journey to share.

However you choose to use the book, my wish is that it empowers you, the reader, to enjoy a happier life in the knowledge that the decisions you make will have been influenced by the highest source of love and wisdom.

For information about my CDs, workshops, to give feedback or query anything about the techniques and approaches in this book, go to www.svaughan.co.uk

Part I

Angels: Our Invisible Companions

CHAPTER 1

Who or What are the Angels

Every time you allow the angels in to your life, you are adding that bit more love and light into our world.

This part of the book will be devoted to our invisible companions: who they are, what they do, how you can raise your awareness of their presence and how once you have opened your heart to the angels how you can enter into a working partnership with them.

Have you been touched by an angel?

Have you ever felt a gentle wind across your face that seemed to come from nowhere? Have you ever been in a situation and thought afterwards "Phew, there must have been an angel watching over me and protecting me"? Have you ever you woken up from a dream and thought you saw something in your room, which perhaps you later put down to your imagination? Well, it's very likely that your life has already been touched by an angel. Being touched by an angel is to be touched by that force that created the angels and all life.

So what are they?

All life forms vibrate at a certain frequency; the heavier the vibration, the denser the entity thereby making it visible. The angels exist on a finer, faster vibrational frequency to our own which is why they are not usually perceived by us with our physical senses but they certainly can perceive us. They are intelligent and sentient beings and because their feminine and masculine energies are in perfect harmony they are androgynous and for this reason are beyond sexual desire. Some people hold the belief that they are the thoughts of the "Divine Mind". The most widely held belief is that they are appointed by Source (God) to act as messengers of light and love who work as protectors and guardians of creation.

Because angels are formed of such a light, fine frequency, they can take any form that is deemed necessary at a particular time. For instance, if they are to intervene in a life threatening situation involving a child, to appear as an immeasurable being of light may frighten that child. Therefore they may appear as an ordinary man or woman. The form they take may be as a lorry driver, a nurse, a man in a pin-stripe suit or an old woman. If we want them to appear to us with wings, they will have wings. No matter what their appearance, they have an aura of peace around them and those who have been touched by such an angel encounter will have the feeling that they have been blessed in some way.

They have been with us since the beginning of time. Ever since Humankind was painting pictures on cave walls or telling stories, he has made images or given accounts of these heavenly beings.

What do they do?

The word angel is a generic term for all of the heavenly beings in the angelic hierarchy. Some of them are closely concerned with helping and serving humanity and Planet Earth. There is an angel to watch over virtually every aspect of our activity: creativity, our careers, families and finances. There will be an angel who comes to us when we are married or totally committed to a relationship whose task it is to help the couple stay and grow together. There are angels who watch over planets, suns, whole solar systems as well as countries, cities and towns. There are also angels that preside over cultures, organisations and governments.

Our guardian angel is our closest companion and is assigned to us as we are born into our lives and they are there at our deaths to help us return to spirit. In between they protect and guide us with their wisdom and love throughout our lives. We will take a closer look at these celestial protectors in Chapter 4.

Our most powerful resource

In contacting the angels, we open ourselves to a level of wisdom and understanding that we may rarely be able to access ordinarily. As a result, we will receive more of those intuitive flashes which let us know when we are in the right place at the right time or conversely if we are about to take a wrong turning in our lives. The angels are our most powerful resource. Their capacity for love and compassion is beyond our wildest imaginings of what love and compassion could be. Their wish is to help us and they are waiting patiently for us to open our hearts to them and ask for that help. Whenever you involve the angels in your life by asking for their assistance in making a difficult phone call, giving you the courage to go to the dentist or asking them to protect a loved one, you will feel their presence around you.

Quite naturally, I have asked for their help in writing this book and each time I sit at my computer to write as I am right now, I feel them with me. My experience of their presence is warmth around my shoulders and a heady combination of buoyancy and quietness. I wish I could bottle this feeling! Everybody has their own experience of their presence. A friend of mine feels a tickle in her nose and a deep knowing that they are there. Someone else I know feels warmth in their heart area.

They are here, there and everywhere

Angels can be in an infinite amount of places at once so don't think that you will be stopping them doing something "more important" when you consider asking them for help. They are more than willing to assist you in the mundane tasks in your life as well as the big projects because the more you allow their guidance to help you along your life path, the more you will come to understand that your relationship with them is really the most natural thing in the world.

The result of this will be freedom from any of the restrictions and limitations you may have been caught up in before. You will come to understand that you are never alone or unaided. There is always help and guidance at hand. Another important point you could contemplate is that every time you allow the angels in to your life, you are adding a little more love and light into our world.

They are here and now

The angels are closer to us now than ever before. Perhaps the reason for this is that there are more and more people raising their awareness of their presence. We all have access to them. They are just waiting for us to make their acquaintance. Contact with them is not confined to the elite few that are initiates of a religious order as was the case hundreds of years ago.

My earliest childhood memories are of feeling their loving presence around me and holding me tight. I would lie in my bed as I prepared to go to sleep and feel their comforting love. It is such an incredible joy to me now that there are so many books written about them, programs made and articles in magazines. There are images in the form of pictures, jewellery and ornaments which help to serve as reminders of their presence. All of this is broadcasting the message that they are here, now and ready to help us as soon as we have the humility to do so.

Have a chat with your angels

To be with your angels, you don't always have to be in a candle-lit room in deep meditation; sometimes there just isn't the time. All you need is an open heart. When I am walking into town to do my shopping, I often have a chat with them (out loud if no-one is around). Sometimes it may be to ask them to send their light and love to someone who is sick or in need. At other times I may ask them to help me cultivate patience, willingness or some other quality I may need for a particular situation. As I set out on a long journey in the car I always ask the angels to help me to drive with a watchful eye and a steady hand whilst driving and perhaps an easy parking place when I get there. Below are a couple of examples of how they can help.

Example one: my marketing

Whenever I feel my practise needs a little boost of clients, I have always asked the angels in "HQ" (Heavenly Quarters) to do a little marketing for me. I say something like, "Dear angels, if there is anyone that would really benefit from the skills I have to offer, help them to hear about me in some way; help them notice my advertisement, allow that leaflet tucked at the back of the drawer to surface or perhaps encourage them to share their health concern with a friend that can recommend me. Thank you." Then I simply let it go and know that it is in their hands. Whenever I book a new client in the diary, I always look up and say "Thank you".

A friend of mine who was just starting out as a practitioner called me one day saying, "I have been advertising for a couple of months now and I'm just not getting any enquiries. What do you do for your marketing?" I passed on to her the above and three weeks later she called with, "It really works! My advertisements are now bringing results." I congratulated her and in enquired whether she had remembered to thank the angels for their help. She admitted she hadn't but promised to as soon as she was off the phone.

In our scientific age, many believe that if you can't see it, it doesn't exist. There will never be any instruments with which you can see them but that doesn't prevent all the wonderful accounts that are told about their miraculous interventions in many people's lives. Many of these relate that the angel appeared to take on a human form to assist them in some way and the following account is one of them.

Example two: a heavenly holiday rep

I have always encouraged my daughter, Rhianon, to call on help from the angels whenever she needs it and the following experience was certainly a time to do just this. Rhianon had decided to go "flight only" to Fuerta Ventura for a week's holiday. She intended to find accommodation when she was there. Her reasoning was that there was bound to be tourist information at the airport. There was no such thing. She walked out of the airport, looked around and still no information kiosk in sight; just a few bus stops going who knows where. She looked up in desperation and said, "Please, angels, help me. I'm really in a spot. What am I going to do?" Seemingly from nowhere an aged hand appeared and pulled her to one side. It was an old Spanish woman who pointed over to a bus stop and told her in broken English to take a particular bus to a village and to stay at a certain guesthouse.

Rhianon thanked the old woman and walked across the road to where she had been directed. Halfway across the road she looked back to wave to her and found that the woman had completely disappeared. She seemed to have vanished into thin air. There was nowhere for her to have gone. It was flat land with no buildings or trees and she certainly looked too feeble to have made it to the airport in so short a space of time. That would have required a rapid sprint.

Rhianon followed the old woman's instructions of how to get to the guesthouse that was suggested. It was here that she met a young man who had had a similar angel experience the day before. He had met someone on a beach who, out of the blue, gave him some very relevant advice on a particular issue in his life and then walked on leaving him a little awestruck. Rhianon's new friend also turned back to say "Thank you" and, just like the old woman, she had vanished into thin air. The two of them teamed up each evening at the beach to enjoy the beautiful colours of the sun setting on the ocean. She met all sorts of interesting and spiritual people on that holiday and said that it was like being on a meditation retreat. She maintained the "old woman" who directed her there was definitely heaven sent.

Aids to focus your awareness of the angels

The angels are there to help us to reconnect with the Source and there are many ways to do this. Meditation is an excellent way and I have given some suggestion later in the book. There are also many Angel Cards that are available that you can use. You can use the cards whenever you need to call on the angels for guidance on particular issues in your life or just pick one for the day and meditate on that one card. A dear friend of mine brought me a perpetual flip calendar by Doreen Virtue, "Messages From the Angels"[1]. Every day there is a beautiful illustration of an angel with a short except from the book of the same title. It is a great way to start the day; flipping the calendar and looking at the "thought for the day". Images of angels around your home will help too.

Celebrate with the angels

The angels can share your joys as well as your sorrows. Invite them to be with you when you celebrate your successes, your birthdays and anniversaries. At a wedding ceremony there will be many angels celebrating the union of two people in love and they could be even closer if invited and acknowledged. G K Chesterton once said "Angels fly because they take themselves lightly". Laughter certainly can be a wonderful therapy. Norman Cousins in his book *"Anatomy of an Illness"*[2], tells the story of how he cured himself of a disease affecting the connective tissue which the doctors considered irreversible. He was not prepared to accept this depressing diagnosis and decided to boost his immune system with high doses of Vitamin C and laughter. He booked himself into a hotel and played loads of Marx Brothers videos (before the days of DVD). He literally laughed himself back to health.

You could celebrate just being alive. Invite the angels to join you in watching a beautiful sunset, when you are laughing, dancing or being with those you love. We can take ourselves lightly and fly with the angels.

Dare to believe

If you find it hard to accept the concept of angels, experiment for a week with assuming there is a loving, powerful presence around you. Try acting "as if" it is there. If you cannot believe or feel the love that the angels have for you, pretend that you can. Imagine the love to be greater than you have felt extended to you before, that it is nurturing you, protecting and guiding you. If you have a difficult task, act "as if" you have an angel or even a whole host with you whilst you perform it and see how it feels. You might get a surprise. Sherwin Nuland, author of "*The Wisdom of the Body*" [3] who teaches surgery and the history of medicine at Yale, once said that "the essence of being a sceptic is not just to question everything and anything, but to believe that anything and everything can be possible" and that is how he feels about angels, God and an afterlife. Anything is possible.

Your imagination can serve as a doorway to receiving the angel's unconditional love. This wonderful energy of love can heal your life and help to transform our planet. So allow yourself to feel it; relax into it. Love is the energy that holds the universe together. All you need to do is dare to believe.

CHAPTER 2

The Angelic Hierarchy

The angels provide the bridge between humanity and the Source of All That Is

The following system is taken from the writings of Dionysius the Aeropagite and is the one most commonly followed in the Western world. Dionysius was a convert of Paul's in the first century A.D. who died a martyr's death. His writings became well known in the sixth century but it is thought that they are largely derived from an oral tradition passed down many centuries before being written down.

The Source of All That Is radiates divine energy and this energy emanates outwards becoming light. As this light emanates further from the Source it becomes heat and finally sets into matter. It is helpful to think of these emanations as concentric circles of energy and it is within these that the angels reside. In the Dionysian system there are three choirs or spheres of angelic beings which are each sub-divided into three, the closest to the Source being the first choir.

The first choir

The first choir is the most powerful and purest of all consisting of the seraphim whose being is love, cherubim whose function is knowledge and thrones (or wheels) whose eyes are all-seeing. The seraphim are the first emanation from the Source and constantly sing the praises of the Creator. This "song" maintains the vibration of all creation. They are angels of selfless love. They are usually depicted with six wings. There is a pair of wings that cover the feet with which they can move between heaven and earth. With the pair that is outstretched they can move the first and second choir of angels and with the pair that covers their eyes they move between the first choir to the Source. The seraph lives in all worlds supporting the aphorism that "Love knows no boundaries".

The cherubim are the guardians of light, the stars and wisdom. The divine light of their wisdom filters down to form. They are associated with the Greek word "Logos" of which the nearest translation is "word"; the word of God. They are usually depicted with four faces looking in four different directions.

The thrones are guardians of the planets. They are often depicted as having many wheels or eyes. They are in essence the eyes of God.

The second choir

The second choir work as heavenly governors and is composed of the dominions, virtues and powers. The dominions govern all the choirs of angels further out from the Source than they are. They act as heavenly administrators. Although they rarely have any direct contact with us, they work to integrate the worlds of spirit and form. They are channels of mercy and forgiveness.

Virtues send out massive levels of divine energy that is available to us. This energy can cause miracles to happen. It can remove obstacles. When groups strive for a just cause, they can tap the energy of the Virtues to fuel their cause. They will also aid the individual struggling on their own against injustice. The more that we connect with the angels, the more we can allow the spiritual energy of the Virtues to infuse our planet.

Powers are the bearers of human conscience and hold the records of our history. The Lords of Karma are one and the same as powers. They are the angels of birth and death. They lovingly help our transition from spirit into form and will guide us back again in to light. They reconcile opposites; harmonising good and evil, light and dark, joy and sorrow, love and hate. When we are in form we are subject to duality and it is the function of the powers to harmonise the apparent contradictions to form a higher unity.

The third choir

The third choir function as heavenly messengers and is composed of principalities, archangels and angels. Principalities are guardians of all large groups: countries, cities, multi-national companies and governments. They work to encourage global consciousness.

Archangels lead bands of angels and oversee the larger fields of human projects. The four we are most familiar with are Michael, Gabriel, Raphael and Uriel who are most closely connected with Earth. Michael means "Who is like God" and is probably the best known of all the angels. He is the guardian of peace and harmony. He is always depicted with a sword symbolising truth. Raphael means "Healed by God" Raphael is the guardian of our physical bodies and healing, of transformation and growth.

Gabriel means "God Is My Strength". Gabriel is the angel of hopes and dreams and of all heart connections. Uriel means "Light or Fire of God". Uriel is the guardian of the mental realm of new beginnings. There are probably millions of other archangels with different functions such as Metatron who is the recorder of the Book of Life. He helps us find the right measure for all that we do and in so doing assists us to fulfil our true potential as loving beings.

Angels are closest to us and we will be most familiar with them as they are most concerned with our affairs; the closest of all being our guardian angel. They are different kinds of angels with different functions such as those imbued with certain qualities such as the Angel of Peace or the Angel of Healing. There are those angels who overlight marriages or careers.

The angels provide the bridge between humanity and the

Source of All That Is. This bridge is formed by different kinds of consciousness that create the various hierarchies. The first step on this bridge is our angel self which we will look at in the next chapter.

CHAPTER 3

We are Both Angel and Human

At our essence we are angel wrapped in our humanity.

I once thought it was necessary to deny my humanity in order to walk a spiritual path. I now know that it is only by embracing it; by learning the lessons it offers me that I can truly make contact with that part of me that is pure spirit. Each of us is angel and human and we pulsate between the two with every breath. At our essence we are angel wrapped in our humanity.

Our angel self

Our angel self is our highest echelon of being. Some may call this the divine spark, Christ self, our higher self or higher consciousness. It is the part of us that has never left the Source. Our angel self connects us with our guardian angel and all the angelic hierarchy to the Source of All That Is. We simply need to quieten the inner chatter and relax into our angelhood and allow the contact to be made. When you do this it can feel like you've arrived home after a long day's work and sinking into your favourite comfy chair feeling relaxed, safe and secure.

In the schoolroom

Recognising our angel self does not mean rejecting our humanness. It is being in human form that we live the adventure and learn the lessons along the way by remembering who we really are. This is the schoolroom. If you want to know if you have any "stuff" you need to deal with just pinch yourself. If it hurts, you have. All the time you are here on earth, there will be some kind of lesson to learn, resistances to clear or emotions to heal until the school bell rings and you don't need to be here any more.

Where is it?

So where is this angel self? There is a theory becoming more widely accepted that it can be found in the space between the sub atomic particles of matter which compose our bodies. Each atom in our body is like a microcosm of a solar system. The electrons of the atom spin around the nucleus in the same way the planets orbit the sun. The outermost planet gives the boundary of the solar system but there is all that space in between. It is the same with the outer electron in that it forms the outer edge of the atom and again with a great deal of space in between. Our physical body is made up of trillions of atoms. If it were possible to take all the space out of our body we would be about the size of a walnut but we would weigh just the same. Our bodies are 99% space. I once read that an atom with seven electrons spinning round the nucleus is analogous to seven wasps in Waterloo Station. That's an awful lot of space! It is within this space the angel self exists.

Find it within and you'll see it in others

Your angel self needs you to be its organ of awareness. Without you becoming fully conscious, your angel self cannot manifest its light, love and wisdom in the world. If we trust our true selves (for that is what our angel self is), then we can trust in life's processes more and develop more meaningful relationships with other people.

We can also make our lives more fun and exciting. We can trust that it is okay to play, to be joyful, to love and be loved. The more we acknowledge the presence of our angel self within us, the more we will recognise the same presence behind every pair of eyes we see. Then the miracles really start happening in our lives!

It is right here within us

We spend so much of our lives looking for fulfilment out there and yet it is really right here within us. There is an old Hindu fable about the gods deciding where to hide man's divine spark.

One thought the bottom of the sea would be a good place, another thought the top of a mountain and yet another the middle of the largest desert. These were decided against as they thought that human beings were such inquisitive creatures they were bound to find it in any of those places. They eventually decided if they were to place it inside us, it would be the very last place we would look. How true. However, it is there within us and all we have to do is look.

Remembering who we are

When we feel fearful, angry, sad or hopeless it is because we have forgotten who we are; angels in human form. I feel that enlightenment is simply the moment of remembering. This may take a lifetime or just a split second. The areas which we may regard as negative are simply portions of ourselves which have forgotten that we are a spark of the Source of All That Is. The Source is where we came from and it is where we are to return in full remembrance at the end of our journey.

Self-love is the key to remembering our angelhood; loving and accepting who we are right now. You will not be able to receive the love of the angels or another person until you love yourself. How else would you feel that you deserved it? How else could you allow yourself to be loved? Self-love opens the doorway to a real sense of union with our angel self.

Also know that when we laugh, shed tears of joy or love, feel compassion, excitement or enthusiasm, we are with our angel self. Our mission is to blend both parts of our being. It is then we can learn through joyfulness and delight instead of suffering.

A meditation to help you remember:

Close your eyes… and relax… nice deep easy relaxing breaths… and just breathe yourself down into a nice quiet place inside… Allow yourself to imagine that your angel self is literally wearing the loose garment of your humanity... Get an image or feeling of your molecular structure... not as dense matter... but light and spacious... only just enough stuff to lightly drape your spirit...

Now imagine the pores of your skin as openings through which your radiant angel self can shine out into the world... Feel that light shining out further and further ... go on... even more... This is who you are... an angel... no limits... remember... and rest a while in your remembering... you chose to enter a tiny little body... you also chose to forget who you really are... but you, the angel, have no boundaries... have not forgotten... and when you are ready open your eyes...

Does the room look different? How do you feel? Are you a little lighter?

Let your light shine

Scientists have discovered there is no point that can be measured at which the light of a candle comes to an end. The light particles get smaller and smaller the further away from the source of the light but it appears that it radiates out into infinity. Hearing about this made me think of our angel self. That also shines out endlessly. We can allow that light to glow brightly in our lives and know it is shining out even further that we can possibly imagine. As our awareness of our angel self emerges, our light easily shines through us and into the world.

CHAPTER 4

Meeting Your Guardian Angel

We can call on them whenever we need protection, help and guidance. They are only a breath away.

Our guardian angels are around us constantly and love us unconditionally. They are beautiful couriers of the Source who accompany us through our lives; all our trials and tribulations, our celebrations and triumphs. No matter how hardened a person's heart may have become, the guardian angel will be waiting patiently for them to turn again to the light. They are our closest companions. Their task is to protect and guide us and will often warn us of danger or when we are getting into situations that are not beneficial to us. However, this warning may not be heard in the hurly burly of our busy lives. This is why we need to still the internal chatter and tune in with them from time to time.

It's a bit like trying to listen to a radio which needs tuning in to the right station. You need to turn the dial and get rid of the static in order to be able to hear what's being said clearly.

We are never alone

They are with us every step of the way whether we are aware of them or not. However when we consciously open ourselves to their love and invite them into our everyday lives, they can help us all the more. They will not intervene unless invited or unless it is a life threatening situation. They will also not intervene if it were to interfere with our free will.

Children will be more aware of the angels up to about seven years of age. They will often see, hear and feel them. After that the memories of angels will often fade and as we grow older and our relationship with them will change. As adults, we need to consciously connect with them.

Receiving help, comfort and guidance from the angels has always been a very down to earth reality for me and not one I have ever questioned. I have enjoyed a conscious connection with my guardian angel since the age of three years. As a child I felt that it was far too cheeky to talk directly to God and the "correct" thing to do was to tell the angels what you wanted help with and ask them to pass the message on.

It was a very long time before I discovered that the word "angel" actually means messenger. I would always know when they were present because I felt that warmth around my shoulders which I thought of as an "angelic cuddle" and would hear a sound that was unique to their presence. Unfortunately I don't hear the sound now but I remember it as being similar to a beautiful chord being played over and over again. It would lull me into sleep.

The angel's embrace

As far back as I can remember I have called on my guardian angel when I feel the need for a little comfort or a cuddle and it has never let me down. An angel's embrace feels like their loving wings are wrapped around me and I feel safe, secure and so completely loved and cherished.

A few years ago, on my return from a shopping trip in London, I got on the wrong train. I started chatting to a charming young woman who was a drama student. I showed her a tee shirt that I had bought in the King's Road which had angel's wings on it and said how pleased I was at finding it because I've always "had a thing" about angels. She replied that so did she and we had the most delightful conversation about angels. She too had felt them with her all her life and told me that she often felt what she called "an angel's embrace". I was so glad to have met her and I feel sure that the angels had led me on to that wrong (?) train. I have since met many people who have experienced being cuddled by the angels. All you need to do is ask them to hold you in their love and you will feel it too.

Carry a reminder of their presence

Find something to serve as a reminder of your angelic connection that you can carry in your pocket. It may be a crystal or a small image of an angel. If not an object, you can carry an affirmation in your heart such as, "Dear angel, I am open to your love and guidance". When you feel fearful or upset you can focus on that special thing and will be able to stand firm wherever you are and feel the fears dissolve. I found an invocation to the angels a few years ago which is a superb way to start the day. *"Angel of God, guardian dear, to whom God's love commits me here, ever this day be at my side, to light and guard, rule and guide."*

Connecting with your guardian angel

When we talk of "connecting to our guardian angel" we really mean raising our awareness of that connection because in truth we are already connected and always have been. Our guardian angel knows and understands everything about us, all our problems and difficulties, all our creativity and potentiality so in tapping into that understanding we can transcend our limitations and apparent difficulties. The connection will allow the joy, love and peace into your heart and will add a little more love into our world. We can call on them whenever we need protection, help and guidance. They are only a breath away.

So here is a meditation during which you can make the acquaintance of your guardian angel. You may want to record this. Alternatively, I have made a recording of it that is available from my website.

Make your self comfortable… take nice, deep, easy, relaxing breaths…   so comfortably there…that   a feeling of peace and tranquillity allows to relax more and more... with each breath... with each gentle beat of your heart... Now imagine a beam of golden light from that Source of infinite love and healing shining down on the top of your head... Now imagine an opening at the top of your head allowing that light to pour into you... filling your body... right down to the tips of your toes... golden healing light... filling every cell and tissue... feel that connection with the Source of All That Is...

Now invite your Guardian Angel to join you... feel their gentle wings enfold you... feel or sense their presence reaching out to you... feel the unconditional love that they have extended to you all your life... Know that you do deserve this love... unconditionally... Breathe deeply and breathe that love into your self... If you wish to ask their name do so... take the first thing that comes into your mind... Perhaps you could ask them to help you feel their presence in some way... be open and receptive to whatever form that takes... it may be a tickle on your nose... a tingle up your spine... or you may see a colour...or a shape... a small or vast being with wings...you may just feel an indescribable feeling of tranquillity... there's no right or wrong way to experience their loving presence... just let go and allow... enjoy... perhaps you could ask them for guidance on a particular issue that concerns you at this time... go ahead... just be open to their guidance in whatever way it comes to you... a voice from them or one inside your head... a picture or a symbol of some kind... don't worry if you don't get a clear message right now... it may come to you later as a flash of intuition... and when you feel complete with your communication thank your angel for their presence... and when you are ready bring yourself back to the room... become fully present in your body ... and in your own time... gently open your eyes.

Do this mediation regularly to help you to open your awareness of your guardian angel and invite them to join you in your life. When I did this meditation many years ago, my guardian angel introduced itself as Aurora. It has been very beneficial to me to have that name to call on when I need to feel its protection or receive guidance.

If we constantly accept the love of our guardian angel we are, at the same time, accepting the love of The Source of All That Is. That love is in a form that is very personal and direct.

CHAPTER 5

Co-working with the Angels

Whatever is created through a partnership with the angels will be done with greater ease and success. You can reach beyond your usual expectation and aspirations.

Co-working with the angels will enhance whatever work you do whether you are a plumber, a stockbroker, a sales assistant or a therapist. If you ask them to be with you in all your activities, your day will be infused with their gentle loving influence. Allow them to become an everyday part of your life and you will notice how much more caring, loving, peaceful and trusting you will become. Try inviting them to be with you while you do the washing up or ironing. It won't be a chore. You'll probably even have fun doing it!

To be a co-creator, simply invite the angels to be with you in your work, your meditations, your dreams, all your dealings with people and things and simply be open to their guidance.

It is for everyone
You don't have to be a spiritual healer, a clairvoyant or medium to have contact with the angels. You just need the willingness to be open to their love. In co-working with the angels we learn to understand that we are never working unaided. They are invaluable assistants to have on board! If we are working with another person in therapy, serving customers in a shop or we have a heart felt desire to help a friend in need, we can call upon the angels and channel their healing energy in whichever form that takes.

Angels in the workplace

After I have been working with a client for a while, they often say they would like to become a therapist or a healer of some kind. My answer to them is always that if you invite the angels into your workplace and give one hundred per cent of yourself to your tasks, you will be a healer to everyone you come into contact with whatever your job title. You will spread light and love wherever you go. So try inviting your angels into your everyday life and watch the miracles start to happen. Ask them to guide your hands if you are doing something that requires skill, help you to assimilate important information, ask them for insight into all your dealings with people or focus your thoughts if you need to concentrate.

For many years in my professional life, co-working with the angels was pretty covert; I would silently invite the client's and my guardian angel to be present during the session to assist with the therapy and to provide me with the insight I needed to offer the appropriate treatment. Co-working became an integral part of my therapy when I made the delightful discovery that when the client also invited the angels and were conscious of the process, the magic can really begin. Whatever is created through a partnership with the angels will be done with greater ease and success. With their guidance you can reach way beyond your usual expertise.

The angels have unconditional love for us, boundless compassion and never-ending gratitude to the Source of All That Is. In developing these three qualities we will help the angels enter into our lives so much more easily.

Love

It starts with you. Loving and accepting yourself just the way you are does not mean you don't want to grow or better yourself. It just means you accept where you are now as being where you need to be. It is being gentle and kind with yourself. It means when things go wrong, extending to yourself the same kind of understanding you would give to a close friend. Loving yourself will help you extend love to others.

Love is not simply a noun. It is also a verb. We allow love to flow into actions. Love in action is a skill which needs to be learned and practised. We devote our lives to it much the same way as an athlete devotes his life to training every day to excel in his field of activity. Some days it may seem more difficult than others because of old habits and patterns of behaviour still clinging on but we keep practising. We are patient with ourselves and others. We may make mistakes sometimes but we will always learn from them.

If we know someone who is suffering, a simple but powerful act of love would be to ask their guardian angel to wrap their loving wings around them. Our love will pave the way for angels to shine their light into their lives. The path of love will reveal our angel self. It is, most probably, our ultimate purpose in being here; to learn to love ourselves and each other.

If we are ever unsure of the right course of action, we can always ask ourselves, "What would be the loving thing to do/say in this situation?" We think before jumping into action. We become conscious of our emotions, thoughts, motivations, preferences and behaviour in order to see more clearly the choices we can make. Love is not something we have to earn, something we give, withhold or take away. It is what we are and is how we communicate with the angels because that is what they are - pure love.

Compassion

When we are kind and loving with ourselves, we naturally cultivate compassion for others. As we grow in awareness of ourselves and our environment, we start to respond to the needs of others. We begin to wonder what we can actually do to meet those needs and how we can alleviate suffering. We move out of isolation and into an awareness of the interdependence of the human family. The prefix *com* means *with* so loving service is not done to others but with. Compassion essentially requires that we are with the person we may wish to help just as the angels are with us. If we feel compassion for another we do not help from an elevated "better than" posture. Being with them we can enter into their perceptions. This way we can begin to accept and understand the motivations for their behaviour. Without this understanding or at least the earnest desire for it, we cannot reach out in love.

When we are compassionate, we are no longer separate from others. We respect the uniqueness of each personality. We let go of any "better thans" or "worse thans" and see the suffering of one person as suffering of the whole. Compassion develops a healthy relationship with our world. Whenever you think about someone, especially with whom you have an attachment or feel any kind of polarity with silently state, "You are a child of All That Is and as such you are my brother/sister". If you are experiencing any kind of emotion which is not love, you will feel it soften as your heart opens. In the case of members of your family, it will help you to look beyond the familial ties to a broader reality. Try it out. You can substitute "All That Is" for "Universe" or "Higher Power" or "God" or whatever is more meaningful to you.

Gratitude

As we develop the quality of gratitude, the more easily blessings can pour into our lives and the more open to angelic influence we will become. I was once on a ten hour flight to San Francisco with a lot of time on my hands and the phrase "counting your blessings" came to mind. I closed my eyes and did just that; allowed the awareness of all my blessing to gently drift to the surface. The more that I thought of, the more came floating up. It was a wonderful process. As each blessing came to mind, I silently gave thanks to the angels and the Source of All That Is. When I opened my eyes I was astonished to realise that two hours had gone by! I felt so joyful and realised then that gratitude is the soil in which joy is germinated.

Saying "Thank you" is a good habit to get into. It is only good manners after all. The angels will always answer your requests for help and guidance however indirectly.

They can also help whilst you sleep

While we sleep the unconscious is open to the influence of the angels. The usual resistances and blocks that may interfere with our connection with the angels in our waking state are temporarily gone. We can facilitate this by inviting them to help us as we settle ourselves down in readiness for sleep. Whenever I am going through a period where I am processing a lot of "stuff", I call on the angels at bed time to request they assist my unconscious to make the adjustments necessary for that particular situation and help me release any resistances to love or forgiveness I may have. Whenever I do this, I have the most amazing dreams so I know something is happening. Perhaps you can say something like, "Dear angels, please will you help me find clarity on …" or "Please will you soften my heart towards …" or "How do I…?" You may even want to write your request on a piece of paper and put it under your pillow. Keep a notepad by your bedside and jot down any thoughts you may have when you wake up.

Prayer is not entreaty

True prayer is not a shopping list of wants and needs. That would separate us from the Source. For me, prayer is like phoning home. It is a deep remembering of who I really am; a piece of the Source of All That Is. Our prayers are already answered the moment we offer them up.

I shall end this part of the book by passing on an affirmative prayer which has proved to be a powerful one for many people. I have given this prayer to people who have telephoned me a few weeks later with amazing feedback such as, "After months, finally the house has sold" or "At last I've found the job that is just right for me". Try it out:

Thank you, angels,
for clearing the obstacles in my path
and creating miracles in my life.

Part II

Getting Started

CHAPTER 6

Basic Muscle Testing

This part of the book will provide you will all you need to get started with KA. The first thing you will need is to become familiar with is muscle testing. If you are already acquainted with it, you can skip this chapter and go on to the next one on silent questioning.

The basic premise behind muscle testing

Kinesiology is primarily defined as the use of muscle testing to identify imbalances in the body. It is using the body as a "bio-computer" to indicate priorities in the treatment of conditions indicated by the use of muscle testing. It also recognises that there are flows of energy within the body which relate not only to the muscles but to every tissue and organ contributing to make the body a living, feeling being. In this way muscle testing can tap into energies that the more conventional modalities overlook as it looks beyond symptoms. It is a fact that 85% of doctors in general practise in the US use kinesiology for diagnosis.

The physical/psychological/spiritual parts of the body know what they need and do not need in order to return to or maintain a balanced healthy lifestyle. It is the innate wisdom of the body. Together, our body, mind and spirit create an environment that, when balanced, is strong and solid. If something enters that environment and challenges the balance, the environment is weakened. That strength or weakness first registers in the electrical system, and it can be discerned through the muscle-testing technique. You can also use muscle testing on your pets and children by using someone as a surrogate. We will look at this in Chapter 17.

Step one

The most common way of muscle-testing is to use the extended arm, as a kind of lever; held out perpendicular to the body; arm held out to the side with palm facing down. It is testing the shoulder adductor muscle. The tester will push in a downward motion in order to weaken the muscle with the other hand resting lightly on the shoulder of the arm you are testing. The other person holds the muscle tightly in an attempt to stop the arm going down. Whether the subject is standing or sitting down doesn't make any difference - whatever is easiest. Give the instruction to, "Push up to the ceiling" and test by exerting a downwards pressure.

Don't be too quick to push as you may override the test. Count a silent 1 – 2 – 3 whilst gradually feeling the resistance. This will give the other person's unconscious time to process the request.

Step two

Pass your hand in a downwards direction a few inches away from the person's body (as if you were unzipping them). This appears to temporarily cut through the electrical field of the body causing the muscle to weaken (the arm can be pushed down easily) and then test. It will test weak now. It will stay weakened for about 7 seconds unless you carry on to step three.

Step Three

"Zip" them back up again by passing your hand upwards in front of their body and test again. It should test strong again now.

The reason for finding out if the muscle will weaken is so that if someone is testing strong, it is relevant to the test you are doing. It is not, for instance, because of a hypertonic (frozen) shoulder muscle. Sometimes a client will test weak consistently because of dehydration. If it's a hot summer's day and this seems to be the case, I simply give them a glass of water and continue.

General Tips on muscle testing

Always give clear instructions; i.e., "Push up, back", etc and don't rush things otherwise you will override the test. Throughout your testing procedures, aim to be consistent in the pressure you exert. Practise as much as you can to gain your confidence in muscle testing. Also practise muscle testing on different people so that you get used to differing muscle strengths. If you are doing a lot of testing the testee's arm will get tired. Ask them to tell you when this is the case so that you can swap arms.

P.S.

Apart from applying it to KA techniques, muscle testing can be useful to test for food intolerances by simply asking someone to hold the suspected food and muscle test. If they weaken it is an indication of an intolerance of some kind. In Appendix ii, we will look at allergy testing and clearing in more depth.

You can also test for the dosage of supplements. Ask the person to hold on to a number of the pills/capsules and test. If it tests weak take one out and test again. Keep doing this with the amount until they test strong. They will test weak on too much *or* too little and will only test strong on the exact amount.

CHAPTER 7

Silent Questioning

Once you feel comfortable with your basic muscle testing, try this first exercise:

How certain emotions weaken the body
This experiment shows clearly how negative emotions can affect us:

- Apply the three step procedure as set out in the previous chapter. 1). Test. 2) Unzip/test. 3) Zip up/test.
- Ask the person you are working with to close their eyes and think of the last time they felt angry or resentful.
- Wait until they have accessed it. You will see Rapid Eye Movement (eyes moving under the lids), change in pallor, muscle tension, etc.
- Muscle test. It will test weak how ever hard they try to resist.
- Ask them to think of something up-beat and happy. They will test strong again.

Silent questioning
This next exercise is just a bit of fun but it will prepare you for techniques later in the book. It is a bit like using the body as a lie detector. You can silently ask the other person questions and you will obtain accurate answers. This is because it is the person's unconscious which will answer and at the deepest level of our unconscious we are connected. Carl Jung, the renowned Swiss psychologist, called this level the "collective unconscious".

Step One

Write down a list of ten questions. Don't tell your partner what you have written. Make sure that each question can only have a definite "Yes" or "No" answer. No maybes. I give a list of example questions below.

Silently ask these questions one by one, test and put Y (testing strong) or a N (testing weak) beside them.

1. Do you live on Mars?
2. Are you married?
3. Is your name Doris?
4. Do you have two legs?
5. Do you have a car?
6. Have you got a parrot?
7. Have you got any sisters?
8. Are you female?
9. Are you male?
10. Have you got a banana in your ear?

Add more of your own to get used to the way you do silent questioning. Have fun with this but one thing I will emphasise here is to NEVER ask a silent question that you do not inform the other person about. It is highly unethical.

I first discovered the efficacy of silent questioning when I was still a student of kinesiology. I was considering the idea that we are all one at the deepest level of our being and decided to try out some silent questions with my daughter as an experiment. I wrote down ten questions like the ones above which could only elicit "yes" or "no" answers and tested. We got ten out of ten right so I went on to another ten and another and another. I eventually tested one hundred questions with one hundred per cent correct answers!

This exercise will help you begin to understand the process of using the body as an oracle. In Chapter 11 we will be using this technique this to access the wisdom of the angels.

CHAPTER 8

Inviting the Angels

Practice quieting your mind and asking to feel your angel's love and presence on a regular basis. They are with you whether you are aware or it or not. In Chapter 3, I used the analogy of tuning in to the radio. The more you tune into the angels' frequency, the easier it will be to find the "Angel Station".

It is important to understand that each one of us has an inherent ability to connect with the angelic realm. Their help is there for each one of us and we already possess the tools we need to communicate and receive information from our invisible helpers. We just need practise. Try out the suggestions in this book then experiment with others until you find the way that is right for you.

That extra "oomph"

When you want the angels to work with you, all you need to do is ask. If it is for the highest good of the other person, they will be there for you. They will give what ever you do that extra "oomph". This is my favourite way of connecting before working with a client:

With your feet flat on the floor take some nice, deep, easy, relaxing breaths... allow yourself to become still... Imagine that infinite source of love and healing above your head... and feel that love pouring down on the top of your head in the form of golden light... Now imagine an opening at the top of your head which allows that golden light to pour into your body... breathe it into yourself... filling your whole body... Now on your out breath allow it to pour out from your heart towards the person you are working with...

affirming that you wish to be a pure channel for love and healing and wisdom... Invite your guardian angel and theirs and any others angels or archangels that may be able to work with you to help this person... and just rest in the stillness for a while...

This needn't take long and there is no definite "right" way of doing it. This can also be a powerful meditation for absent healing. In this case, imagine that other person in front of you and feel that light spilling out from your heart and flowing towards them until they are totally whole and healed.

CHAPTER 9

TAKING THE REGISTER

Invitation

Using the meditation in the last chapter or one you feel more comfortable with, invite yours and their guardian angels and you could perhaps also invite any other angels that may best be able to help with the particular issue you are working on. You may feel it would be helpful to invite the guardian angel of the person with whom they may be in conflict or dissonance. When two people marry or are in a special relationship there is an angel assigned to the marriage/relationship so it may be relevant to invite this angel too. There are angels who help with romance, healing, career, creativity, family and, yes, even parking (but we don't need to worry about them here).

You may want to invite an archangel

Invoking Archangel Michael will help in seeing the truth about situations, self and others. His sword will cut away old patterns of behaviour that are no longer relevant. His sword symbolises truth and can cut away all falsehoods and those things in your life that can be let go of.

Archangel Raphael's light will assist with self-healing and with healing others. Invoke Raphael for healing on any level whether it is healing of physical ailments, depression, and anxiety, from addictions or the effects of abuse. He is the spiritual source behind all healing. Opening to Raphael will lead the way to the right healers or physicians.

Invoking Gabriel will assist getting in touch with someone's intuition and awaken new aspirations; will assist them to live your truth and find the right path to follow. Gabriel will heal the damaged inner child. Gabriel will also help to mend a broken heart.

Invoke Uriel to invite the power of self-transformation, re-birth and infinite possibilities. Uriel can bring the cleansing and purifying fire of transformation to issues such as work, creativity, innovation, organisation and toxins. Uriel will also help to trust the Divine plan.

It's okay, as I said in Chapter 1, angels can be in an infinite number of places at once so just because these Archangels are high up in the angelic order, don't think you or the person you are dealing with are not important enough to call on their assistance.

Test for their presence

As I am a bit of a "belt and braces" merchant, at the beginning of each session I like to take a "register of angels". I will test, using basic muscle testing whether the client's guardian angel, mine and the angel assigned to the relationship/family, archangel, etc are present and willing to help us.

I will silently ask if my guardian angel is there. If the muscle test is positive (tests strong), I go on to ask if their guardian angel is there and so on. Once they are all in attendance, I will thank them and silently say something like, "Please help me access your love and wisdom in order to help and guide this person".

I feel that warm sensation around my shoulders and a feeling of light-headedness when my angel is near so I know to proceed. You may just sense that they are there. As I've said earlier, everybody has a different experience of the angels.

I then picture them gathered around me and take just a few moments to centre myself in their love before I begin.

Very soon after working with them you will just *know* they are working through you. You will often get feedback from the person you are working with to confirm that it is really happening too.

Part III

Techniques

CHAPTER 10

An Introduction to Kinangiology

So many of my clients and students ask me, "How did the KA techniques evolve?" So I thought it a good idea before we go on to look at them in detail, to give you an account of this.

How KA developed

I started in practise twenty years ago as a hypnotherapist and psychotherapist but after a couple of years, I started to feel a bit lop-sided in just treating the mind. This led me back to college to do a two-year Holistic Health Diploma which covered holistic anatomy, clinical nutrition, iridology and kinesiology.

An abiding interest from this time has been the connection between mind and body. For instance, how hormones affect moods and how moods will affect hormone levels, how blood sugar levels can cause mood swings and how a negative attitude can impair the immune system.

I am committed to the development of holistic health care and empowering others with the attitude and the resources with which they can take full responsibility for their health and happiness. KA has evolved from this commitment. The techniques are a culmination of my years of training and experience as a practitioner.

I worked in a residential cancer clinic for a number of years as well as my other clinics around the country. A significant number of the patients I treated there appeared to have an emotional/spiritual factor contributing to the onset of the disease.

Emotional blocks on the site of the illness could be detected and this led to the development of the Emotional Clearing Technique (Chapter 15) which is a method of identifying an emotional block in the body and provides a way of releasing it I have had truly remarkable results with this technique not only with cancer patients, but with many people of all ages presenting a whole range of physical and emotional symptoms.

I have extended the Applied Kinesiology techniques of Psychological Reversal (Programming Affirmations, Chapter 12) and the Five Minute Phobia Cure (Phobia Clearing Technique Chapter 14) to become far more effective. These with the Emotional Clearing, Chakra Balancing (Chapter 13) and Co-working with the Angels make KA a system which has become an invaluable tool to bridge the mind/body/spirit connection.

I guess if I were to give myself a job title now, the nearest would be "a holistic health practitioner". I have trained in a number of fields in order that I may tailor-make each therapy for the individual.

I have always had a conscious connection with my guardian angel so co-working with the angels felt a natural thing to do. I would always, in preparation to see a client, invite the angels to join me in whatever kind of work I would be doing. This led to using kinesiology to ask the angels questions on behalf of the client and elicit answers (Chapter 11: Using the Body as an Oracle). I have had some extraordinary results using this method to allow the angels to impart their wisdom to help the client find clarity in a problematic situation.

The aim of my work with clients has always been to make myself redundant as soon as possible. I do this is by giving them a whole range of resources and undoubtedly the most powerful resource of all will be connecting them to their angel.

The feedback received from clients and students as well as my insatiable curiosity as to the causes of illness and unhappiness has also contributed to the continued development of KA. In the past many have given responsibility for their happiness and well being to parents, partners, the medical profession or society. KA gives the power and responsibility back to the individual.

CHAPTER 11

Using the Body as an Oracle

Just remember that when you ask the angels, you will always be answered.

Asking any question, especially if we are asking the angels for guidance or help, requires that we open up and reach out in some way. As we open up, we make our self ready to receive in a spirit of acceptance and willingness to listen. This next technique is how to facilitate a conversation with the angels.

Clarify the issue

Firstly it is important to clearly articulate the issue the other person wants clarification on. In the same way as each of the silent questions in Chapter 7 could only elicit a definite "Yes" or "No", the same applies here so elucidation is crucial. Writing it down may help.

Using the oracle

Invite the angels to join you, take the register and you are ready to begin your silent questioning. Only ask four questions at a time before relaying your answers back to the other person as you may forget the answers. If the issue is a relationship one, a useful question is to ask would be, "Is there (still) a spiritual contract between (name) and (name)?" If the question to ask is about some kind of timing it may be useful to ask if it is possible to get clarification on this before you test. If it is, then ask if is within six months, three months and so on until you get a clear answer.

Using KA in this way allows the body to become an oracle for you and your client.

Case history

Linda had suffered with ME for a couple of years and was slowly making a recovery but was still feeling pretty isolated. She had been divorced for a number of years after a difficult marriage and wanted some idea if she was ever to meet her "soul mate".

We asked the angels if there was someone waiting for her with whom she could have a meaningful relationship with. It was a definite "yes" so we asked some more. The answers we received were that she was to get together with this man within the year and it was someone she already knew. She couldn't think of anyone it was likely to be and we forgot all about it.

She is with someone now and he is a warm, loving and considerate man. They are preparing to make a home together and they are very much in love and, yes, she did already know him. They were together for a few months when her daughter reminded her of what the angels had foretold. They had got had got it all absolutely right!

CHAPTER 12

Programming Affirmations

It is useful to determine the subconscious blocks that may be undermining the healing process and in a wider context, the individual's self-development.

Our beliefs create our experience

Everything that has been created by human beings has its origins in a single thought supported by the desire to manifest it in some way. For instance, this book you are reading has its origins in the thought that I could do it, and was carried through by my desire to communicate these ideas to you. However, had I let the voices of doubt that I "could not", "should not" or was "not able to" overpower that seed thought, this book would not be in existence.

As Shakespeare so succinctly put it in Hamlet, "There is nothing either good or bad, but thinking makes it so" (Act 2, scene 2). Affirmations are self-talk. Our self-talk can be positive or negative, life enhancing or those that limit you.

The terrible shoulds

The bogey man of negative self-talk is the terrible should voice: "I should not make mistakes", "I shouldn't complain", "I should be the perfect spouse/lover/friend", "I should be able to cope" and so on. The list can be endless. Freud called this internal voice the super-ego. Others have called it the inner critic/judge/parent. It is the one that gives us a hard time, nags at us, hinders our creativity, spontaneity and very often will drown out the voice of our intuition. It is an amalgamation of all the authority figures that have had any impact on us in our early lives: parents, teachers, priests, maybe doctors and a sprinkling of society's shoulds. They become internalised and the beliefs that are created by this mish-mash of ideas appear to become a part of us colouring our interaction with the world around us. It appears that where our parents finish off giving us our guidelines for life and telling us where we are going wrong, this internal parent takes up the task and will probably be far stricter and authoritarian than they ever were.

One way to find out what affirmations may need programming would be to have a look at what your "shoulds" are. Make a list. If you find it hard, just keep saying "I should ..." and see what comes up and write it down. You may be surprised at the restrictions that are operating below the surface. By looking at your shoulds, you can create the affirmations that you will be able to program with the technique we will be looking at in this chapter.

Psychological reversal

Thought processes play a huge role in a person's health and well-being. There have been those who have been diagnosed with a terminal illness that have survived by changing their thought processes. Sometimes failure to get well can be due to "psychological reversal", a term first used by R J Callahan[1], a psychologist who used kinesiology. Simply put, psychological reversal occurs when a belief in an individual's unconscious mind differs from what is consciously being said. Most people will be psychologically reversed at some time or another in their lives. There may be resistances to success because of the extra responsibilities involved or reservations of being in a relationship because a fear of losing independence.

The following technique in action is a bit like using a lie detector. If someone says something that their unconscious disagrees with, the muscle test will show weak. For instance, if a patient is unwell but has a "secondary benefit" to being ill such as their spouse finally taking notice of them and not taking them for granted, whatever they say about their wishes to regain their health, their unconscious mind may block their healing process in some way. The negative affirmation which may be "running the show" may be something like, "If I get better, things will go back to the way they were. I'll just be a skivvy again".

Another example may be the person who is desperately trying to lose weight (as in the case history at the end of this chapter). If there is an unconscious fear of not being able to handle the attention they may receive from the opposite sex when they are slim, they will almost get to their target weight, panic and subsequently put all the weight back on. This will happen over and over again until this problem has been addressed.

Programming affirmations helps you to replace those old scripts that may have hindered your success. This subtle shift in your mental functioning will have a huge impact on your life. Your new positive attitude will give you confidence and inner strength.

Just one per cent will hold you back

I often say to someone in therapy, "It is probably ninety nine per cent of you that wants to lose weight/get well/give up smoking/let go of the past but the one per cent that doesn't will hold you back from actually doing it". Then, in the spirit of experimentation, we will test for affirmations to see if it is "in the bank". If there is that one per cent in disagreement with an affirmation such as "I am now allowing myself to love and be loved" when you muscle test, it will test weak. It is a very gentle way of revealing what is happening below the surface.

There may well be resistances to working with angels as we do in KA. There may be feelings of not being worthy or not wanting to worry them so this belief definitely needs sorting out.

Testing Procedure

Invite the angels to work with you. Choose an affirmation to work with and ask the other person to say it out loud. In the first example above the affirmation would be, "I want to get well". In the latter example, you could ask the client to say," I now want to lose weight" or"It is safe to lose weight", etc and test. If they test weak, then proceed with the technique below.

Programming affirmations

Ask the person to hold their hands together, palms flat, and repeatedly tap SI3 (an acu-point) of both hands with the outside blade of your hand; like a gentle karate chop whilst they repeat the affirmation about ten times. Use your other hand to hold the fingers together to steady the hands whilst you are doing this. The point is just beneath the knuckle (see illustration)

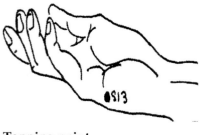

Tapping point

Re-test

You can hear them saying the affirmation with more feeling towards the end of this procedure. I often end up saying "Now once more with feeling" before I re-test. When they now say the affirmation, it will test strong.

Very often, the affirmation that someone literally finds difficult or gets tongue-tied over will be significant. For instance, I once asked a client to say, "I love and approve of myself" and she said, completely unbeknown to her, "I love and reprove of myself" Talk about a Freudian slip!!

Here are a few affirmations to test:

- I love and approve of myself
- I accept myself just as I am
- I am now attracting more and more love into my life
- I am now breaking out of old patterns that restrict my

growth
- I am loved, loving and loveable
- I am now letting go of the past
- I deserve to be happy/successful/loved/appreciated
- I am safe in my world
- I easily release anger and resentment in my life
- I now give myself permission to feel all my feelings
- I am always provided with what I need in life
- I am finding peace within myself
- I am now learning from each new experience
- I am bringing my inspirations to realisation
- I forgive others as I forgive myself
- It is safe to allow myself to love and be loved

There will be more affirmations relevant to the chakras in the next chapter.

Once someone has a little list of affirmations they have programmed, they can tap these in themselves from time to time by holding their hands together and tapping SI3 on the edge of a table.

Failure to get well or be happy or successful may be due to an unconscious self-sabotage. This test is very useful in determining the unconscious blocks that may be undermining the healing process and in a wider context, the individual's self-development.

Case history

Angela came to me for weight loss. She was a yo-yo dieter. One diet after another and every time she almost got to her desired weight, she would pile it back on again. There was obviously an unconscious mechanism at work. When she said, "I am willing to lose weight" she tested positive but when she said, "It is safe for me to lose weight" she tested weak. We knew we were on to something. She tested weak on both "It is safe for me to be slim" and "It is safe for me to be beautiful" and this opened out a discussion as to why she must be feeling unsafe to be slim and beautiful.

Angela had been a teenager in the swinging sixties making "love not war" like most other youngsters at the time. However, Angela had been brought up in a strict Catholic family and suffered a lot of guilt about her promiscuity. She was a petite size 10 until she married when she quickly grew to a size 18/20. The mechanism appeared to be a safety valve to keep her faithful to her husband. If she was overweight she wouldn't be tempted by the attentions of other men. The mechanism had been in place for 30 years and would have stayed in place unless we uncovered it.

When she realised that she really did have the maturity and astuteness to deal with the attentions from men, the mechanism started to dissolve. We asked her guardian angel to take any resistances away for re-cycling and to work with her on her weight loss program.

A couple of weeks later she tested strong on those affirmations about being safe as a slim, beautiful woman and six moths later that is what she became and what she is free to stay.

CHAPTER 13

Chakra Balancing

Each chakra manages different aspects of earthly life: body, instinct, vital, energy, deeper emotions, communication, having an overview of life, contact to spirit.

What is a Chakra?

There are seven main chakras and they are aligned in an ascending column from the base of the spine to the top of the head. They take us from the most fundamental experiences of survival and security at the Base Chakra up to the highest, the supreme state of consciousness, enlightenment, at the crown of the head. Each chakra is associated with a certain colour and an aspect of consciousness. Each will vitalise the physical body and will have interactions of both a physical and mental nature. They act like conductors connecting mind and body are accessed through the spine. They are linked to each of the endocrine glands, which regulate all the various functions in the body.

There are many ways to keep the chakras in balance such as visualisation techniques, the use of crystals, colour therapy and so on. The KA technique of balancing chakras identifies the emotional/spiritual issue connected to a particular chakra. If a chakra tests weak, we find an affirmation associated with that particular chakra and, using the technique in the previous chapter, "tap it in". We will look at the technique in more detail later but first we need to take a closer look at the chakras and what their function is.

The seven chakras and their function

Each chakra manages different aspects of earthly life: body, instinct, vital, energy, deeper emotions, communication, having an overview of life, contact to God. We'll look at each in turn from top to bottom.

• The Crown Chakra situated two to three inches above the head is said to be the chakra of consciousness, the master chakra that controls all the others. It is significant as it provides a channel for spiritual healing and is our connection point to the angels. Its role would be very similar to that of the pituitary gland, which secretes hormones to control the rest of the endocrine system, and also connects to the central nervous system via the hypothalamus (more on this in the Appendix). The thalamus is thought to have a key role in the physical basis of consciousness. The colour associated with this chakra is white. The angel associated with this chakra is Metatron who is the guardian of the Tree of Life linking form with spirit.

• The Brow Chakra, or third eye, is linked to the pineal gland. This is the chakra of time and awareness and light. The pineal gland is a light sensitive gland, which produces the hormone melatonin, which regulates the instincts of going to sleep and awakening. It is the crossover point between intellect and intuition. The colour associated with this chakra is violet. The angel associated with this chakra is Ariel who is the guardian angel of Earth and air helping you to see and hear with your heart.

• The Throat Chakra is said to be related to communication and growth. It is to do with expression of the whole self as well as creativity. This chakra is paralleled to the thyroid, a gland that is also in the throat, and which produces thyroid hormone, responsible for growth and maturation. The colour associated with this chakra is blue. The angel associated with this chakra is Michael will lead you speak your truth.

• The Heart Chakra is related to love of others and self, forgiveness, equilibrium, and well-being. It is related to the heart and thymus, located in the chest. This organ is part of the immune system, as well as being part of the endocrine system in that it produces T cells responsible for fighting off disease, and is adversely affected by stress. The colour associated with this chakra is pink and green. The angel associated with this chakra is Gabriel who brings new hopes, dreams and aspirations.

• The Solar Plexus Chakra is related to will power, control, energy, assimilation and digestion. It is said to correspond to the roles played by the pancreas and the outer adrenals glands; the adrenal cortex. These play a valuable role in digestion, the conversion of food matter into energy for the body. The colour associated with this chakra is yellow. The angel associated with this chakra is Raphael, the healing angel to bring harmony of body, mind and spirit.

• The Sacral Chakra is located about two inches below the navel and is related to emotion, sexuality and our ability to experience pleasure. This chakra is said to correspond to the testes or the ovaries which produce the various sex hormones involved in the reproductive cycle, which can cause dramatic mood swings. The colour associated with this chakra is orange. The angel associated with this chakra is Uriel the guardian angel of fire and alchemy bringing you transformation, creativity and purification.

• The Base/Root Chakra is related to security, survival and also to basic human potentiality. It is our connection to Mother Earth It is said the kundalini lies coiled here, ready to uncoil and bring man to his highest spiritual potential in the crown chakra. This centre is located in the region between the genitals and the anus. Although no endocrine organ is placed here, it is said to relate to the inner adrenal glands, the adrenal medulla, respon-sible for the fight and flight response when survival is under threat. The colour associated with this chakra is red. The angel associated with this chakra is Camael bringing you the energy of courage, passion and confidence.

Testing

Place your hand about three to four inches away from the body at the position of each chakra in turn. If one tests weak, test an affirmation relevant to the chakra (list below). For instance, if it were sacral, the issue may be around pleasure so a suitable affirmation to test could be, "I give myself permission to have fun".

Treatment

Once you have the relevant affirmation, you can balance it by using the Programming Affirmations Technique. Once you've tapped in the affirmation, test the chakra again.

If it still tests weak, keep testing for the appropriate affirmation. Continue testing and tapping in affirmations until the chakra tests strong. Do the same with each chakra in turn until they all test strong.

Now not tomorrow

Sometimes you will tap in an affirmation which seems wholly appropriate but the chakra will still test weak. Often all you need to do is add a "now". It is as if the unconscious can say "I am willing to forgive all past experiences" but there is an aside that says, "But not right now, maybe tomorrow". So try, "I am willing to forgive all past experiences *right now*". The unconscious can certainly be a slippery customer at times!

Affirmations for Balancing Each Chakra

Crown:

"I am now connecting to spirit."
"I am safe in God's hand."
"I am allowing the angels to give me healing."

Brow:

"I now listen to my intuition daily."

"I see and hear with my heart."

"I listen to my own inner guidance."

Throat:

"It is now safe to be me."

"I have something to say and I'm willing to say it."

Heart:

"I am allowing myself to love and be loved."

"I forgive others as I forgive myself."

"I love and approve of myself."

"I forgive all past experience."

"I deserve love/approval, etc."

Solar Plexus:

"I am going with the flow."

"I trust in life's processes to care for me."

"I now give myself permission to feel my feelings."

"I let go and let God."

"I am letting go of the past."

Sacral:

"I deserve to enjoy myself/to have fun."

"I deserve to be happy."

"I can now enjoy a loving and sexual relationship."

Base:

"I am finding security within myself."

"I am centred and grounded."

"I am connected to Mother Nature."

This obviously is not the definitive list. You may have to find a more appropriate one. Look at the emotional/spiritual issue connected to the particular chakra you are working on and work out the affirmation to balance it. It is like being a detective "on the trail".

Case history

When Denise came to me she was suffering from classic "empty nest syndrome". She was in her late forties, kids had left home and had their own lives. For most of her life she had been a mother, a wife, chief cook and bottle washer and was now feeling a bit redundant. Who was *she*?

When I checked her chakras, the only one that tested weak was the throat chakra. We tapped in "It is now safe to be me" and the chakra tested strong.

As the throat chakra is connected to the expression of the self and creativity, I asked Denise in which ways she felt she may be blocking this. She answered that she had always wanted to learn how to paint with water colours but she had never found the time whilst her children were growing up. We looked at ways she could begin to make friends with herself and get her confidence back.

We asked the angels what she needed to do next. On their advice, Denise joined an art class which not only helped her find her creative expression but also provided a whole new social group for her. She no longer feels her useful life is over and is enjoying new challenges in her creative work. She is in the process of producing a set of beautiful greeting cards.

CHAPTER 14

Phobia Clearing Technique

It works because the brain cannot separate visualisation from actuality.

When the only tool I had to treat phobias was hypnotherapy, it was a long-winded affair which would last four to six sessions. The Phobia Clearing Technique has completely transformed my treatment. I have been using it for about sixteen years and, in the majority of cases, it will only take one session of two hours to clear the phobia however long the person may have suffered from it.

This technique and the Emotional Clearing one in the following chapter involve clearing emotions from the meridians so I will start this chapter with a brief explanation of what a meridian is.

What is a meridian?

The body is part of an energy system and the meridians are channels that transmit energy upwards and downwards through the body. Each one is associated with an area in the body. The meridian system is the interface between the energy field and the physical body. There are 12 major meridians each with a beginning and end point and acu-points along its course. Where there are blockages in the energy field, there are corresponding disruptions in the flow through the meridian system.

The technique we are going to be looking at is based on the premise that phobias get stuck in the stomach meridian. Think about it – where is it in the body that you will usually feel fear? Of course it is the stomach. We get those collywobbles or butter-flies in the tummy when we are fearful.

What is a phobia?

The definition of a phobia is *an irrational fear*. This means that no amount of logic and reasoning such as "Flying is the safest way to travel" or "That spider can't possibly hurt me in any way" or "The snake is behind glass so it can't get at me" is going to make any difference at all. A phobia may be directed to practically anything in an individual's day-to-day reality; public speaking, animals, spiders, dentists, flying, heights and so on. Some things like public speaking may be avoided but agoraphobia (fear of open spaces) can literally imprison an individual suffering from it in their home.

Testing

Invite the angels in and ask them for help in clearing the resistances to letting go of this problem and to take the fear away to be recycled. Angels are very green! Ask the person you are working with to close their eyes and think of the subject of their phobia. They need to be associated; looking out of their eyes, hearing through their ears, etc and not dissociated; seeing themselves from a distance in that situation.

Clearing

If weak, ask them to keep their eyes shut and lightly tap on both ST1 points (see illustration below), about twenty times simultaneously. Then ask them to imagine the same thing and test. It will test strong now.

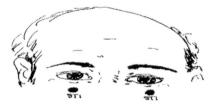

Every step of the way

Very often the phobia will start with the anticipation. For example, a flight phobia may kick in when they are booking the flight, the night before or getting ready to leave for the

Phobia points

airport. At each step of the way you ask them to a) imagine that stage b)test c) if weak, tap as above d)re-test e)go on to the next stage (if it tests strong just go straight on to next).

Flight phobia sequence

A typical sequence for testing and clearing a flight phobia would be:

- Imagine yourself in the travel agents.
- Imagine yourself receiving your tickets
- The night before the flight
- Getting up in the morning
- Leaving the house
- On the way to airport
- Arriving at the airport
- Checking in
- Waiting for flight announcement
- Going through passport control
- In Departures
- Getting to plane (coach and/or tunnel)
- Getting on plane
- Finding seat
- Waiting for take off
- Take off (break this down; taxiing down runway, etc)
- Going to the toilet mid flight
- Turbulence
- Plane banking round to land

You get the picture. You may need to break the steps down even more than this in some cases.

Re-Test

Once you have gone through all the stages; from the anticipation to actually doing it/being there, ask them to close their eyes and visualise the whole scenario as if watching a movie but with them in an associated state. Say, "As soon as you feel any anxiety or collywobbles in your tummy, freeze-frame the picture and let me know". Test, tap the ST1s and re-test before asking them to continue "the movie". Repeat this until they can run right through it without any anxiety.

In many phobias, you will need to test it in various situations. For example, if it is a spider phobia, it may be slightly different going into a room and discovering a spider to turning on a light and seeing one in the bath.

The brain does not know the difference

People often say to me beforehand "But how will I *know* if it will be okay in the actual situation. The answer is that the brain does not know the difference between visualising something and actually doing it. I had been taught this in my psychology studies but it didn't quite sink in until I saw an interesting program about sports psychology on the television a few years ago.

A man was wired up to a machine which was testing the activity of a number of muscles on his body whilst he was running around some cones in a gym. You could see the effect of the muscles on a tracer graph. After a while, they asked him to stand still and visualise himself doing the same thing. Then they showed the two readings one on top of the other. Yes, you've guessed it! It was exactly the same. No difference at all, proving the theory perfectly.

The following case history also illustrates the fact that the brain cannot separate visualisation from actuality.

Case history

Derek was not only phobic about dentists but as soon as a dentist put his fingers anywhere near his back teeth, it made him gag. He was never *actually* sick but he said he felt he got pretty close to it at times. When he came to me for treatment, he was in need of some dental work doing on a back tooth. His dentist could not do what was necessary because of Derek's severe reaction; even visualising the dentist doing this made Derek gag so I had to work pretty quickly.

As in the flight phobia scenario above, we imagined him getting up in the morning, arriving at the dentist, checking in at reception and gradually stage by stage clearing as we went, at the end of the session, he could even visualise himself having a root canal job done on a wisdom tooth without gagging.

Derek wrote to me after his dentist appointment describing how it went. He wrote, "I've had a successful trip to the dentist, which I was able to take in my stride. I can't believe the difference. I've only his charges to worry about now!!"

My own experience of this technique

This technique is useful at times without the muscle testing procedure. I was involved in a traffic accident on a motorway a couple of years ago involving fifteen cars. I had a spinal injury which meant I had to spend two weeks in hospital and then a few months recuperating at home mostly flat on my back. It was eight months before I was physically able to drive but because of the trauma, I was terrified at the prospect of being behind the wheel again. In effect I had to learn to drive all over again. My husband was very patient with me and coaxed into me to driving short distances with him at my side. Every time I came back from our driving lessons I would close my eyes and remember the parts of it that I found difficulty with and tap the ST1 points.

Eventually, I managed to do the journey from my home in Devon up to my clinic in Buckinghamshire which is about 180 miles. I travelled on smaller dual carriageways at first which meant that if I started to feel a little shaky I could easily pull over into a parking lay-by and tap those ST1s, take some deep breaths and continue. I now have my confidence back completely on motorways, dual carriageways and country lanes alike.

CHAPTER 15

Emotional Clearing Technique

The body retains everything it has ever experienced: events, emotions and stresses and strains are all locked in the body.

The jigsaw puzzle pieces

Looking at a health problem holistically, we can see it as a jigsaw puzzle. One piece may be life style, another diet, another environmental, another genetic and yet another may be emotional. We cannot see the whole picture until all the jigsaw puzzle pieces are assembled. I work as a clinical nutritionist, kinesiologist as well as a psychotherapist and see how important all these pieces are in making up a complete picture of a client's presenting problem.

For instance, if I am treating someone for depleted adrenals as well as prescribing something to bring the glands back into balance, I will use the Emotional Clearing technique to test if there are any emotional blocks on the site of the adrenals and clear them. This will be the same if I am treating eczema, arthritic knees, thyroid problems, sluggish liver and so on. I have been following this procedure for seventeen years and I have found in the majority of cases of physical complaints there will be emotional blocks at the site of the affected part of the body. The Emotional Clearing technique has been invaluable in treating the emotional piece of the jigsaw puzzle.

Before using this technique, I felt the same as most people in the Western Hemisphere; emotional memories are in your head and that is where they are kept. Now I understand that they can literally be anywhere. I've even cleared emotional blocks from someone's big toe!

Repressed emotions in the body

Blockages are caused by significant emotional events and an accumulation of constant or repressed emotions. Where these blocks exist, there may be corresponding problems in that area and will manifest in some way. If there is an emotional block, for instance, in the spine, the manipulations by a chiropractor or osteopath may not hold. They will have to keep going back in an effort to correct the problem which could be a costly business!

Many clients have come to me with just such a problem (see case history at the end of the chapter). When the emotional block is cleared at the very least, the manipulations will hold but in many cases the problem clears up completely.

Emotional patterns

We are the sum total of what has happened to us. In clearing these blocks, the trapped energy that may be have been there for most of someone's life is released. With the Emotional Clearing Technique we can begin to understand the messages underlying health problems and begin healing on every level: mind, body and spirit. Because there are often many layers of emotional blocks to clear in one session, there are often emotional patterns that can be detected as these layers are unravelled. For instance, the blocks may be predominantly anger, anxiety or fear of rejection.

In discovering these past patterns of repression, the person can more easily understand their current emotional behaviour. If I am seeing someone over a period of time, different blocks come up at different times. It is like peeling back the layers of an onion Blocks do not come to the surface in a neat chronological order. The only sense I can make of it is that when an emotional block is registering in the body it is ready to be released. The body has wisdom of its own.

Testing Procedure

Invite the angels to take the cleared emotions and recycle them and begin by placing the person's hand on the area of the main organs in the body. If they have or have had particular problems, aches or pains in any area such as spine, limbs, joints, or patches of eczema test these too.

Is this an emotional block?

This part of the body may test weak because of a physiological dysfunction of some kind so to determine if there is an emotional block in that particular area, place your hand over their forehead (there are emotional stress receptors here). If this causes the muscle test to change and become strong, it will be an indication that there is indeed an emotional block. Remove your hand and now you are ready to find out more about how the block was caused.

NOTE: The client maintains contact with that part of the body throughout the whole procedure.

Testing for the age

Emotional blocks may date back as far back as birth (occasionally in womb). They may be due to present concerns. You can test for the age the person was when the significant emotional event occurred.

- "Did this event happen between the ages of nought to ten?" and muscle test.
- If they test strong, break it down to "nought to five".
- If it tests weak, try "five to ten".
- Then break it down to the actual year until they test strong to a particular year.

Remember, the whole time they have their hand in contact with that emotional block the muscle will test weak so the muscle will test strong when you ask the right question and will continue to test weak when you don't. It may be present emotions or before birth (in the womb) so if you have any difficulty finding the age, test for these.

Testing for who or what
To find out who or what it was to do with ask:

- "Is it to do with a particular person?"
- If they test strong ask, "Is it a member of your family?"
- If this tests strong go though the individual members.
- If it is not family, it may be friend/colleague/spouse, etc.
- If it tests weak on the first question it may be (according to the age) something to do with school/ work/ career/ finances so test for these.
- It also may be concerned with the feelings they may have held about themselves.

Testing for the emotion
Then you can test through the whole gamut of emotions. If it is about them, it could be self-doubt. I have often been surprised by love being the cause of a block. It seems to have been when love has been overwhelming in some way.

Clearing procedure
Once you have all the information you and the other person wants, you can clear it from the body via the Clearing Points below. For those interested in kinesiology these points are Hypothalamic Set Points. They are on both sides of the face. If you are unsure which point, you can test for it. Again, as long as the other person is still in contact with the emotional block, if you touch the correct point with a finger tip it will test strong. If it tests weak, keep trying until you find it.

With the person's hand still over the site of the block, tap lightly on the appropriate Clearing Point about 20 times. If the emotional block is on the left, tap the Clearing Point on the left.

The same with the right side. If it is central, tap both points either side of the face. For instance, if the emotional block is in the centre of the stomach, tap both ST1 points. If it is in the middle of the chest, it would be both TH23 points.

Emotional clearing points

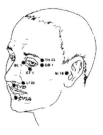

TH23: Thyroid, heart, chest, lungs, eyes, central face
GB1: Gall bladder, liver (left side), adrenals, kidneys, legs, arms, side of face/skull, ovaries
BL1: Bladder
ST1: Stomach area
LI20: Large intestine
SI19: Small intestine
GV25: Hypothalamus (Test in between eyebrows)
CV24: Spine, reproductive organs (central), central skull.

Re-test

Once you have completed the clearing procedure, re-test. That area will test strong now. There may be yet another layer on that same site so wait a couple of minutes for it to surface and test again.

The effect of self-talk

The way we "language" ourselves may go towards creating our physical reality." It makes me sick", "This job is such a headache", "You've broken my heart", "Thinking about this problem is just eating away at me", "He is a pain in the neck/backside". The following case history is a good example of this kind of self-talk.

Case history

Stephanie had a sharp pain in her right gluteus maxima (backside). She had been to a physiotherapist for months before she came to me in desperation. At each session, the physiotherapist managed to clear the pain but it would return within the hour.

We tested for emotional blocks and, sure enough, we found about twenty layers of blocks concerning her ex-husband with whom she had recently gone through an acrimonious divorce. One after the other, we cleared the layers of resentment, anger and sadness. Her ex-husband was literally a "pain in the backside" as far as she was concerned! In fact, she said just that before we started clearing the emotional blocks.

CHAPTER 16

Cross Pattern Treatment

The period between the ages of six months to one year is when the mid-brain develops. This is known as the *Cross Pattern Stage.* This is a time when the child develops the ability to use both sides of the body together and co-ordinate bodily function such as the hand with the eye. At this time the child learns to use arms and legs together in a *cross-pattern* motion. This means flexing the arm and leg on opposite sides while the other arm and leg is extended. The right brain controls the left side and the left controls the right so crawling requires both sides of the brain to work together. This is an important developmental stage and will prepare the infant for an upright position.

Causes of disturbed development
This may occur because of brain injury or any kind of disease that may interfere with normal nerve function. Freedom of activity is essential at this time so restriction by confining children in rigid carrying baskets, playpens, walkers or even bulky nappies or clothes if worn frequently might cause disturbance in development. When a child breast-feeds, one eye and arm are alternately restricted as the mother swaps breasts from time to time. The bottle fed baby is usually fed in the same direction which will restrict one eye and arm. Other causes may be forcing a child to stand and/or walk prematurely or attempting to change a normally developing left-dominant child to a right-dominant one. During mid-brain development, eating with both hands enhances bilateral function.

Another cause may be emotional trauma. At the seminar where I first heard about this syndrome, I tested weak at the first hurdle. I had always been calculus dyslexic so I was not unduly surprised. At coffee break, I was chatting to a colleague and expressed a curiosity as to whether emotional trauma may also be a contributory factor as I had been adopted at ten months old. My colleague had also tested weak and said that his father had died during his mid brain development. When we re-entered the seminar room we contributed these thoughts and there was a chorus around the room of others that were either dyslexic or had one or more of the symptoms below and had also suffered emotional trauma of some kind during this stage of their lives.

Symptoms
- Illegible hand writing
- Poor spatial awareness
- Poor co-ordination (clumsy)
- Poor hand-eye co-ordination
- Dyslexia
- Calculus dyslexia
- Getting left and right confused

Testing Procedure
Ask the individual to walk on the spot with arms swinging (like a soldier marching). Once they have got a good rhythm going, ask them to turn their head and look over their right arm as it comes up. Muscle test.

If that tests strong, have them look over their left arm as it comes up. Muscle test.

You can make it more refined by incorporating eye movements with the head. The exercise that tests weak will usually give the person you are testing a feeling of "spacing out", almost vertigo like sea sickness.

Correction
The exercise to correct the disorganisation is the one that tests

strong *not* the one that tests weak. This is to be done for 10 minutes for approximately 3 weeks and re-test the one that tested weak. If they test it out themselves without you they will know it has cleared if they don't get that "spacey feeling".

Case histories

In my maths classes at school, I would space out and not know why. Phone numbers were always a trial as I would very often get them back to front. Adding up more than two figures was almost impossible without a calculator. After following the above procedure, this has improved greatly. My calculus dyslexia will only return if I am stressed or tired so at these times I need to go back to the above procedure to keep it established. I am also a lot less clumsy these days. I can juggle now whereas before I was very "butter-fingered".

An eleven year old boy was brought to me suffering with allergies but whilst he was there his mother mentioned that he was dyslexic. At the end of the consultation, I used the cross pattern treatment with him and we established the right exercises for him to do for the next few weeks. When I saw him a month later he tested strong on the exercise he tested weak on so we went on to make the testing procedure a bit more complicated; he looked right round to the right as he looked over his right arm and the same the other side. Again his exercise was the one he *could* do.

He was already finding his dyslexia a lot more manageable but six months later his mother rang me up to say that there was a marked improvement. On his school report the comments were that there was improvement in his spelling, better co-ordination in rugby and his hand-writing was more decipherable.

CHAPTER 17

Surrogate Testing

I first used surrogate testing when I was working as a kinesiologist/clinical nutritionist in a private hospital. There were many elderly patients who were not strong enough to undergo muscle testing. I would enlist the help of one of the nurses to act as a surrogate. The patient would lie on the therapy couch and the nurse would hold their hand or lay a hand on the patient's shoulder. I would then muscle test the nurse. For instance if I was testing for allergies, I would ask the patient to hold on to one of the ampoules in my allergy test kit and then muscle test the nurse.

I know this sounds strange, but it does work. The reason for it is that the energy of the testee passes through into the surrogate. I once conducted an experiment (at a Christmas party) with a group of seven people who were all holding hands. One was seated and the rest were standing in a line alongside each other. I muscle tested the person furthest away from the seated one. They tested strong. I then quickly moved along to person seated and "unzipped" them and moved back to the surrogate testee. They tested weak. I ran back to the seated person and "zipped" them back up again and tested the surrogate at the end of the line. They tested strong again. After this, I asked the person seated to think of something that made them angry as in the experiment in Chapter 7 and tested the surrogate. The surrogate tested weak. The anger went down the line! Cause for thought.

How does it work?
The energy of the testee passes through into the surrogate. If two people hold hands and the first person sticks his finger in an

electrical socket, it will only be the second person who would get electrocuted not the first. I don't suggest trying this out but many years ago I was walking over the fields with a group of five friends and somebody raised this theory when we came across an electric fence. After much heated debate over who was going to be the experimental creature on the end of the line, I drew the short straw! However, it proved the theory. Nobody else felt a thing. It was only a tingle but energy certainly passed down the line.

Testing on pets, animals and children

Think of a surrogate as a human energy conductor. If you are testing a child, the surrogate maintains some form of skin-to-skin contact with them. The muscle testing is done on the surrogate who holds the child's hand or in the case of a baby they can cradle them. The child can even be sleeping. It is useful if you are working with children especially if very young or uncooperative such as those that are autistic, have ADHD or the severely injured. You can do surrogate testing on your pets too.

KA surrogate testing

As far as KA techniques are concerned, I have used *Chakra Balancing* with a surrogate. You place your hand over the chakras of the person to be tested and test the surrogate. If one tests weak, ask the person to say one of the affirmation and if it tests weak, you tap it in on them and use the surrogate to test if it is "in the bank".

In the case of the *Emotional Clearing* technique, the person places their hands in the way described in Chapter 15 and test the surrogate. If it is weak you place your hand over their forehead to ascertain if it is a block and continue with the clearing. You tap the points on their face and the surrogate is simply there for the muscle testing.

In *Using the Body as an Oracle* you can ask silent questioning but naturally if you are to relay the answers they need to trust the surrogate to be witness to this or you can tell them after the session when you are on your own together. You will have to write it down as you go in order to relay it all. The same may be done with an animal that is unhappy for some reason. You can ask the angels for information that will help the owner help their pet.

CHAPTER 18

KA Dowsing

All the KA techniques we have looked at in this book have been using kinesiology. This obviously means you cannot do it on your self. However, some of the techniques can be adapted for use with dowsing; using a pendulum. With a pendulum it goes round one way for *Yes* and the other for *No* in just the same way as you get a strong or a weak muscle. First for those who are new to dowsing, I'll outline the basics.

Introduction to Dowsing

A dowsing pendulum is an object suspended by a cord, used for obtaining information. You could improvise with an everyday object such as a pendant on a chain. However, a purpose made pendulum is best because it has a shape, geometry and weight. This allows the swing to be more constant and sensitive and therefore more effective.

When choosing a pendulum/crystal make sure it has a good weight and balance. If it is too light you may not get clear responses. The Yes/No technique is most common in pendulum dowsing and is what will be most appropriate for KA. Experiment with this until you feel comfortable with it. Hold the pendulum cord between thumb and forefinger about three to four inches above the pendulum and let it hang more or less motionless. Ask a question mentally for a reaction to the answer *Yes*. Wait a few seconds for a reaction, which could be one of the motions described below. Your concentrated desire for a yes response will have impact.

Again, let the pendulum hang and mentally ask for a reaction to the answer for *No*. The pendulum should move but in another manner or direction. The fingers and arm should not be held rigidly. The idea is for any movement to be unconscious and not directly influenced by wishful thinking. Be patient.

Possible directions of the pendulum

A. Clockwise/circular right
B. Counter-clockwise/circular left
C. Diagonally left
D. Side to side
E. Diagonally right
F. Back and forth

Various reactions will be obtained by different people, male or female, as well as left or right handed, and you should be able to establish your own way. For example, some people find A to be yes and B to be no or vice versa. Others find yes to be C and no to be E, or vice versa.

Any combination of these examples can do. You will find your own natural preferences, which may be best for you as, after all, it is the accuracy of results that count. For those using a pendulum for the first time, don't worry if you do not get a consistent reaction or if you don't get reaction at all. A little practice will produce results. Be patient and don't force it.

KA Dowsing

Here are some general guidelines for adapting the KA techniques for dowsing:

Programming affirmations

Holding the pendulum, say an affirmation and wait for the movement of the pendulum. You may need to say it two/three times. If the pendulum indicates a "no" response, put your hands together (in prayer pose) and knock the SI13 points (Chapter 12) on the edge of a table. Alternatively you could just tap one SI13 on one hand against the SI13 on the other whilst you repeat the affirmation. Then dowse to see if it "is the bank".

Chakra balancing

Holding the pendulum in one hand, place the other about 2/3 inches away form the body over the chakra areas and wait for a response. If a chakra tests weak, choose the appropriate affirmation as above, tap it in then re-test the chakra. This is a wonderful method of daily maintenance for your self development.

Emotional clearing

Whilst holding the pendulum, place your other hand on various parts of your body (especially if you have an ache or pain somewhere) and wait for a response. If an area tests weak, find out the when, why and what. All the time you have your hand over the area, the pendulum will go one way and when you say the appropriate age it will go the other. If it doesn't change, keep asking until you get the right one. The same goes with who or what it is to do with. Once you have all the information you want to know, put the pendulum down and, keeping your hand over that area, tap on the appropriate Clearing Point. Test again.

A word of warning

I do not advise using dowsing for asking questions of the angels. Wishful thinking or a preconceived outcome, however slight, can be magnified making the use of the pendulum in that instance ineffective.

As you become more open and co-work with the angels and the communication channel between you and them becomes more established, they will become an everyday part of your life making everything you do a meditation. Your intuition will become heightened as a result. You will get more and more of those intuitive flashes letting you know an angel is tapping you on the shoulder and saying "Don't go there" or "Do that" or "Phone them".

CHAPTER 19

Putting it all Together

So you've learned all the techniques. Now it's practise, practise and more practise. Just remember the magic ingredient with all the techniques is to co-work with your invisible friends. Just keep asking for their help and guidance every step of the way. They will be only too glad to help you with all your work; they are waiting.

When I am working with someone on emotional or physiological issues, I always start with the Chakra Balancing technique. I then go on to clear any emotional blocks. This always opens up a discussion about what happened to them at the significant emotional events that caused them. Talking about those things will often bring up more blocks (the layers of the onion) to clear so I will re-test.

Once there appears to be nothing left to clear, i.e., everything tests strong, I usually ask the client to join me in silently asking the angels, "If there is anything that could be cleared today that would be helpful for this person, please allow that emotional block to come to the surface to be cleared". Then I test again. Without fail, there will be more. As I've said earlier in the book, they are wonderful assistants to have on your side! When these have been cleared, I go back to the chakras to make sure these are all testing strong.

I don't consider myself to be a clairvoyant or clairaudient in my everyday life. I am intuitive because I have been a health practitioner for twenty years but when I co-work with the angels my intuition is so much sharper and extends well beyond my normal capacity. I access wisdom that is not just mine. So can you.

If you are doubtful any step of the way if you are doing it right, email me via my website. Details are at the front of the book.

APPENDICES

Appendix I More KA Case Histories

Here are some more case histories illustrating the use of KA in order that you can get a clearer idea of the use and benefits of the techniques in this book.

A bridge phobia

I had been invited to Wales to do a KA workshop. A close friend of mind, Karen said she would like to do the workshop and so suggested that she drive us there. Around this time, Karen was doing an awful lot of driving in the course of her business so she was a very confident and competent driver. During the journey we were chatting, having a sing-song to an album by Carole King and generally having a relaxed time getting there.

However, when we started to go over the Severn Bridge Karen suddenly stopped talking and looked as if she was concentrating very intensely. It was so out of character that I asked her what was going on. She simply replied, "I'm driving on a bridge over water". I tried not to distract her whilst we were on the bridge because she was obviously distressed. Once we were on terra firma the other side of the River Severn, I asked her what the problem was. She replied that she was always panic stricken when she was driving over bridges that were spanning water.

I commented that she was certainly coming on the right course to deal with that and asked her to call me over in the workshop when we came to the phobia clearing to make sure that her bridge phobia was well and truly cleared.

We had a great weekend; the workshop was a success and our Welsh hosts were extremely hospitable. On the return journey, we were halfway across the bridge and I remembered about

Karen's phobia and asked her if she realized where she was. Her reply was "Yes, we're on the Severn Bridge. So what?" It was as if she had never had the phobia.

A few weeks later we went by train to London to do some sightseeing. After our day in the big city, we were about to walk over a pedestrian bridge across the River Thames when Karen froze and said, "I can't go on the bridge!" The phobia about *driving* over bridges had been cleared but not *walking* over them. So right then and there with crowds of people passing by (but not taking a blind bit of notice), we cleared it and walked over the bridge enjoying the view.

Bird phobia

Mike came to me to clear his bird phobia. He had had it since he was a small child and the phobia had extended to include anything that flapped such as washing on a line or curtains blowing in a breeze. Even the feel of feathers in duvets, pillows or feather cushions was quite distressing. It had limited his life so much because whenever he went to stay with people he always had to make sure he wasn't going to be sleeping under a feather duvet and birds, well, there are always a lot of those around.

There were a lot of different scenarios to test and clear. At the end of a session, I put a feather cushion in his hand and that was fine. I then took him outside to watch the birds. He was delighted and even enjoyed watching them fly.

Balloon phobia

This next case history is from the first time I used this phobia clearing technique. A mother booked her eleven year old son in for a balloon phobia. As you can imagine this phobia was really restricting his life. He couldn't go into McDonalds as there are always balloons in there. Parties and shopping malls were also no go areas.

I was completely honest with him and his mother in that I had not used this technique before. I told them that if it didn't work, she could bring him back and we would book him in for a series of hypnotherapy sessions and I would not charge her for the first one. Anyway, I used the Phobia Clearing Technique and asked his mother to ring me the following week to let me know how things were going.

His mother called me and said, "Listen to this". All I could hear was a lot of pops, bangs and whoops and yells of "Yeah!" He had bought a packet of balloons blown them up in his room and was in the process of stamping all over them with glee. All I could say was, "So I don't need to see him again?"

This certainly disproved any idea that you need to believe in something for it to work. I hadn't really given them much confidence in what I was doing but it worked all the same.

Emotional clearing

Debbie was being treated for digestive problems. During the Emotional Clearing procedure, we discovered a block at the age of twenty one and the person it was to do with was one of her three daughters. When we tested for each one of the girls it ensued that it was Sophie. This confused Debbie because Sophie had not been born until a year later. I checked and re-checked the age and who it was concerning and it just kept coming out the same. I ended up as confused as she was. A few moments later, Debbie looking a bit overwhelmed said, "I know what this means and I've never told a soul about it".

She went on to explain that she had suffered a miscarriage that particular year and had always believed when Sophie was born, she was the little person that she had lost come back to her. We tested if this was the case and it was. Debbie was visibly lighter and with tears in her eyes told me that she couldn't wait to tell her husband. It certainly sent a shiver up my spine and still does in remembering it.

Programming affirmations

Christine came to me for help in giving up smoking. I use KA in adjunct to hypnotherapy for smoking cessation just in case of that unconscious one percent that does not want to give up. We started our session by testing for the affirmation "I am now willing to give up smoking". This tested weak. Whilst we were tapping it in she got a little tearful and told me that whenever times were tough, she was lonely or just needed a friend, cigarettes were always there for her. The thought of letting them go was frightening; like saying goodbye to a dear and faithful friend. We realised that they had been an important emotional resource up to now. If she felt happy, she smoked. If she felt sad, she smoked. If she felt lonely, she smoked. If she felt anxious or depressed, she smoked. Basically, they were a way of helping her not feeling her feelings; a smoke screen against them.

When I checked her chakras, the solar plexus was testing weak and the only affirmation that strengthened it was, "I now give myself permission to feel all my feelings". There were no tears this time. In fact she said she felt as if a weight had been lifted from her. Bringing all this to the surface enabled us to look at other ways for her to manage her emotions; walking, soaking in a candle-lit bath, yoga, playing her guitar and so on. She could now find more satisfying options of behaviour to replace her smoking. New resources with which to deal with her emotions. She felt empowered with these new choices and implementing these she felt that she could let go of the cigarettes gladly. She realised that cigarettes had become the lazy option. We then went on to do the hypnotherapy to encourage these new behaviours at the unconscious level.

The most difficult thing concerning addictions of any kind is the emotional dependence. This kind of re-programming will help to clear it. I feel sure that hypnotherapy alone could not have achieved this as effectively.

Martin, Joe and Theresa are all ex-students of mine and their experience of using KA illustrates how it can blend with other therapies.

KA and Aromatherapy

Martin is an Aromatherapist who feels that he could not achieve the same results without the integration of KA into his practise. Basic muscle testing helps him to select the most appropriate oils but the emotional clearing helps him to clear the underlying emotional problem that may be causing the physical tension his clients may be experiencing.

James, 35, came to Martin with tension in his neck and shoulders. He had suffered from this much of his life. His doctor had been unable to help him apart from the offers of painkillers and muscle relaxants such as Diazepam, which he was reluctant to take. When he came to Martin for help, the discomfort was causing him to have to take time off from work. After testing for the right oils, Martin gave him an aromatherapy massage to relax him and to identify the tense areas in his body.

After this Martin carried out the Emotional Clearing technique and discovered that there were layers of emotional blocks he had been carrying from childhood. He seemed to have been carrying the weight of the world on his shoulders. After three sessions his neck and shoulder muscles had loosened up enough for him to go back to work.

KA and Neuro Linguistic Programming (NLP)

Theresa is an NLP Master Practitioner and Hypnotherapist who finds the Emotional Clearing and Chakra Balancing techniques provide clear information about what kind of emotional patterns have been/are being repressed and in so doing helps her to choose the most appropriate NLP procedures. Using the Body as an Oracle helps her to give the client the direction they seek for the future. She has completely abandoned her old method of treating phobias in favour of the KA Phobia Clearing technique as it has proved more effective and less time consuming.

KA and Osteopathy

Joe is an Osteopath who finds the KA Emotional Clearing invaluable in cases where clients have recurrent or persistent structural problems. In fact now he uses it as part of his initial consultation and has found that his work has become more dynamic and effective as a result.

Sally had been recommended to attend Joe's clinic almost as a last resort having been to physiotherapists, doctors and back specialists of all kinds over the years but still suffered from crippling pain in her lower back. Joe found many layers of emotional blocks going back as far as birth. He cleared these and did some osteopathic manipulations. Each time he saw her, there were more emotional blocks and he cleared them and manipulated her back. He felt that the manipulations were loosening the trapped emotions so sometimes he cleared emotions, manipulated then went back to clearing emotions and so on for maybe an hour. After six sessions, she was completely free of pain and stayed that way.

All three have also said that they really noticed the difference in their work with clients when they requested assistance from the celestial A Team.

Appendix II Allergy Testing & Clearing

I vacillated as to whether to include this particular Appendix but in the light of the fact that allergies are now such a major health issue affecting many people, I felt it important that this technique is more widely recognized. Approximately one in four of the population in the UK at some time in their lives will suffer from some kind of allergy and that number is increasing every year. Many of those affected are children whose symptoms may include behavioural problems.

Now you are used to the basic muscle testing you can use this technique to test and clear allergies. I use this on people with hay fever, food and contact allergies.

What is an allergy?

An allergy is an immune system reaction: the immune system is over-reacting. An allergic person's immune system believes allergens to be damaging and so produces a special type of antibody (IgE) to attack the invading material. This leads other blood cells to release further chemicals including histamine, which together cause the symptoms of an allergic reaction.

The term allergy is used to describe a response, within the body, to a substance, which is not necessarily harmful in itself, but results in an immune response and a reaction that causes symptoms such as itching, headaches, intestinal pain, coughing, sneezing, diarrhoea, rash, sinus problems, sweating, runny nose, etc. In young children they can cause behavioural problems. The substance in question is known as an allergen.

What causes an Allergy?

Almost anything can be an allergen for someone. The most common allergens are:

pollen from trees and grasses, house dust mite, moulds, pets such as cats and dogs, insects like wasps and bees, industrial and household chemicals such as cleansers or air fresheners, medicines, and foods such as milk and eggs. Less common allergens include nuts, fruit and latex.

When someone's immune system is compromised for any reason; virus, prolonged illness or stress, allergies occur even if the individual has never suffered before. I have found that top of the list of culprits in the case of skin problems; rashes, eczema, etc will be soap powder and fabric conditioner. Even if you have been using the same one for years, the formulation will have change; new "colour brightener" or "white whitener" and so on.

Testing

I use a whole barrage of test kits for allergens but you can just gather up the suspected food stuffs, bottles of cleansers, samples of soap powders and test them. Ask the individual to simply hold the item and muscle test. If it tests weak do the clearing. If it is for animal hair, put a sample of the fur in a plastic bag to test. If you want to test pollens, put an open jam jar of water in the garden for a few days. The pollens and moulds in the air will be attracted to the water. It will be like an "essence of garden". Put the lid on and test with this. A client of mine who suffered more in the winter put a jam jar for a few days in various rooms in the house and brought it to my clinic. I don't know what it was but when we cleared it, his symptoms disappeared and that is all that matters.

Clearing

Place allergen on the area just above the navel and tap on the points indicated below. It doesn't matter what order. These points are the beginning and end points of the major meridians of the body and this appears to re-program the body into accepting the substance Tap each point on each side of the body about 15/20 times and re-test.

The points on the face: at the beginning of the eyebrow, ST1 (see Chapter 14)

On the body: on the outside crease of armpit, central to armpit at level of nipple.

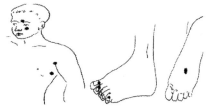

Allergy clearing points

On the feet: on the inside corner of big toe nail, at base of second toe nail, base of little toe nail, central in the hollow just below ball of foot.

Appendix III Mind/Body/Spirit: The Science Bit

Psychoneuroimmunology

Psycho - mind/emotions Neuro - nervous system Immunology - immune system.

Psychoneuroimmunology (PNI) is the fastest growing field in the healing arts. It is the study of how negative beliefs and emotional states can affect the immune system; how it is that people with an optimistic outlook, positive expectations and high self-esteem tend to have fewer illnesses.

The brain and the immune system speak the same language. Neurotransmitters, hormones and other chemical messenger molecules once thought to be restricted to the brain are now known to be active in the immune system. Conversely, certain immunotransmitters and other chemical messengers once thought to be exclusive to the immune system are now known to act on the endocrine and central nervous systems.

Lawrence LeShan in his book *"You Can Fight for Your Life"* , when asked if anxiety can lead to serious illness, said, "Many medical investigators contend that there is hardly a major illness that cannot be triggered by profound anxiety. Depression and despair make their registrations not just in the mind but in the body". We are expressing these more hidden and denied messages all the time without being aware of them and these unconscious energies can permeate our whole selves: mind, body and emotions.

If we talk about someone being a "pain in the neck" or our "heart being broken", the body will not understand the metaphor. However, messages that are based on hope, love and a joy of living are those that encourage the physical self to build up its strength and vitality. Thomas C Haliburton (1796 - 1865), a Canadian politician, judge, and writer once said, "Cheerfulness is health; the opposite, melancholy, is disease".

The hypothalamus

The hypothalamus is often called the "great communicator" because it is the crossover point between the endocrine system and the nervous system. It organises whole entities, which we see as acts of behaviour. For example, the hypothalamus alters the rate and depth of breathing rhythms when it is organising running away, fighting, sleeping or waking up. It will also govern the breathing rate when strong emotions are felt.

The Vegas nerve from the hypothalamus connects directly to the stomach which is why stomach and stress are often closely linked. Other nerves from the hypothalamus are connected to the thymus and spleen which in turn make the immune cells and regulate immune function in the blood.

The hypothalamus controls the appetite; it informs the body when you are hungry, when you are full, what tastes nice and what does not. There are what is known as "reward centres" in the thalamus, hypothalamus and parts of the cerebral hemisphere. Because the hypothalamus registers pain and pleasure, it is associated with eating disorders, drug and alcohol addiction and perhaps obsessive compulsive behaviour.

The limbic system

The limbic system incorporates the hypothalamus and has two main functions. Firstly, it regulates autonomic functioning such as fluid balance, gastro-intestinal activity and endocrine secretion. Secondly, it integrates the emotions. The input for limbic activity seems to come directly from the cerebral cortex, which is the part of the brain which is responsible for all intellectual activity: memory, thinking, perception and interpretation. It is often been referred to as the "seat of the emotions".

The cerebral cortex will sound the alarm in a situation that is *perceived* as life threatening (it may or may not be in reality). The alarm signal then affects the limbic/hypothalamus system, which in turn affects hormone secretion, the immune and nervous system. When we suffer severe stress, the hormones released by the adrenals (triggered by hypothalamus) suppress immune system functioning. The hypothalamus controls the autonomic nervous system and the endocrine system of the body, and in turn they affect many parts of the brain.

All we experience and all we hear can influence the whole of our nervous systems and secondarily of our bodies. The awakening of emotions, the reliving of experiences and re-awakening of memories have effects on our personalities and behaviour and will affect the cerebral hemispheres.

Everything we have experienced and has made us what we are has entered our brain through some sensory channel: skin, eyes, nose or ears. Much of it will be via the ears in the form of speech. And so there is no reason why further talking; i.e., therapy, should not continue to affect us and influence our personalities.

It is the close relationship between the hypothalamus and the cerebral hemispheres, which makes NLP, psychotherapy, hypnotherapy and talking to a good friend so helpful in our self development.

Appendix IV A-Z of Emotional Causes to Illness

While you are doing your KA work on the body with the Emotional Clearing Technique, this brief A-Z may be interesting to you. It will give a possible clue as to how the significant emotional event that caused the block may have become stuck in the body.

Addictions: Fear of feeling emotions

Adrenals: Letting go of the past. Fear. Trauma.

Allergies: Insecurity, anxiety.

Ankle: Ability to support ourselves. Blocked energy to/from earth.

Arms: Holding back from reaching out with heart energy. Skin: frustration with what we are not doing.

Arthritis: Rigidity of thinking, repressed resentment.

Back: Where we put everything we don't want to look at (turn our back on), the past.

Upper back: Anger, resentment, resistance to/fear/rejection of love.

Middle back: Resistance to maturing, conflict with authority, ego.

Lower back: Resentment and frustration Sexual conflict, financial insecurity.

Bladder: Irritation, Hurt and anger we are holding on too (pissed off!) Relationships.

Bowels: Ability to let go and surrender.

Breasts: Nurturing or lack of. Shame. Mother issues. Left: Acceptance of being a woman, mother. Right: Being a woman in the world, what is expected.

Chest: Identity, inner part of our being. May hide real feelings here.

Colon: Assimilation, resistance to change, self-worth.

Diaphragm: Resistance to breathing deeply, taking in life.

Ears: Inability to deal with what we are hearing, conflict in some area. Balance.

Elbows: Restriction of movement of expression and creativity, confusion of expressing heart energy.

Eyes: Windows to the world and to our soul. How we see life and relationship to it. Ignoring present and dreaming about future.

Face: Putting on a good face, a mask.

Feet: Ungrounded, insecure in relationship to world, conflict with direction life is going.

Fingers: Reaching out too far.

Gall bladder: Rage, fury, wrath.

Genitals: Sexual abuse, mistrust, fears fear of own potency, shame.

Hands: Cold – withdrawal from world. Hot/sweaty – overabundance of emotion, anxiety. Cramp – lack of a grasp of reality Arthritis – rigidity, lack of spontaneity.

Head: Cutting self off from body, conflict between experience and expression.

Heart: Grief, loss, "heartache".

Heartburn: Fear

Intestines: Not assimilating new ideas, experiences and hanging on to negative emotions.

Jaw: Stubbornness, anger.

Joints: Resistance/irritation to movement – maybe fear of what lies ahead.

Kidneys: Holding on to old emotional patterns/fears. Relationship issues. Stones – unshed tears.

Knees: Lack of humility, flexibility, conflict with authority, arrogance.

Legs: Not making a stand for self, lack of direction, purpose.

Liver: Stores repressed anger.

Lungs: Grief, feelings about self.

Mouth: Conflict with expression and ability to say what is meant and what we are taking in.

Nails: Resistance to change.

Neck: Inability to see from all sides, extreme stress causing wish to withdraw and close in.

Nose: Life is overwhelming, difficult to deal with.

Ovaries: Ambivalence about expressing femininity, motherhood.

Pancreas: Inability to express and integrate love throughout whole being, anxieties for future.

Pelvis: Reluctance to share self though sex, move in new direction in world or inner realm.

Prostate: Frustration, confusion about sexuality / performance / power.

Ribs: Weakness, vulnerability, helplessness.

Shoulders: Carrying responsibility, burdens, not happy with what we are doing. Frozen shoulder: Giving/receiving "cold shoulder", indifference to someone, rather be doing something else.

Skin: How we think other people see us, how we see ourselves, vulnerability.

Spleen: Overwhelming emotions, sadness.

Stomach: Digestion/assimilation of life/reality. Nurturing.

Teeth: Gateway through which reality must pass. Unacceptable reality.

Testicles: Powerlessness, doubts about masculinity.

Throat: Problems with communication, expression of whole self. Holding back emotions.

Uterus: Anxieties about womanhood and ability to create, betrayal.

Wrists: Arthritis – critical attitude to what we are doing or being done to us.

Wrist pain: Repressed energy about something that needs to be done.

REFERENCES

Chapter 1

1 Virtue Doreen, Ph.D., *"Messages from Your Angels. Perpetual Flip Calendar"*. Hay House, Inc. 2005.

2 Cousins Norman, *"Anatomy of an Illness as Perceived by the Patient"*. W. W. Norton & Company, New York, London. New Ed edition 2005.

3 Sherwin B Nuland, *"The Wisdom of the Body"*, Chatto and Windus, London. 1997.

Chapter 12

1. Callahan R J *"Psychological Reversal"*, Proceedings of Winter Meeting, ICAK, Acapulco, Mexico, 1981. as cited in: David S Walther, DC, *"Applied Kinesiology, Synopsis"*, Systems DC, Colorado, US, 1988.

Appendix iii

1. Le Shan Lawrence, *"You Can Fight for Your Life: Emotional Factors in the Treatment of Cancer"*, M Evans & Company, Ltd, 1980, US.

BOOKS

O books

O is a symbol of the world, of oneness and unity. In different cultures it also means the "eye", symbolizing knowledge and insight, and in Old English it means "place of love or home". O books explores the many paths of understanding which different traditions have developed down the ages, particularly those today that express respect for the planet and all of life.

For more information on the full list of over 300 titles please visit our website
www.O-books.net